Hulks

To MARK,

I HOPE YOU ENJOY IT!

[signature]

Hulks

The Breakwater Ships of Powell River

John A Campbell

🍁 Works Publishing

Powell River, BC Canada

Book design, layout by Robert Dufour, Works Publishing
Printed and bound in Canada

Cover art: "The Hulks" by Joanne Clark, *Stillwater Studios,* Powell River

This project was made possible with the support and encouragment of NorskeCanada, Powell River

National Library of Canada Cataloguing in Publication

Campbell, John A., 1955-
  Hulks : the breakwater ships of Powell River / John A. Campbell.

  Includes bibliographical references and index.
  ISBN 0-9687351-8-5

  1. Ships—British Columbia—Powell River—History. 2.
Breakwaters—British Columbia—Powell River—History. I. Title.
VK26.C35 2003   387.2'09711'31   C2003-910879-1

To the women in my life:

My mother, Winnifred,
My wife, Brenda,
And my daughter, Jessie.

Contents

Acknowledgements

I would like to thank the many people who contributed so much to this book:

From NORSKECANADA, Powell River Division, Ed Doherty, for buying into the project and supporting its publication. Karen Crashley, Michelle Powell and Karen Thom for allowing me to explore the dusty files in the company archives for documents, drawings and photographs that had not seen the light of day for many years.

From the NORSKECANADA Millennium Project, Emma Levez Laroque, for what must have been hours of reading, editing, and suggesting improvements, and Juania Swanson, for saving many digital images for my collection.

From the Hulk's Reconfiguration Project, Mike Pedersen, one of the few people to sail aboard one of these vessels — even if it was only across the log pond! — for sharing his findings and expertise in the technical aspects of concrete ships, and for finally getting me aboard.

Maritime researchers, Frank A Clapp, whose files must be considered one of British Columbia's maritime heritage treasures, and Rick James, the acknowledged expert on BC's ship breakwaters, for the continual flow of information during the research for this book.

Teedie Kajume from the POWELL RIVER HISTORICAL MUSEUM, for allowing me free access to the photographs and files in the archives, and Leonard McCann of the VANCOUVER MARITIME MUSEUM for allowing me access to the photographs and files in their collection.

All of the Powell River residents who contacted me with stories about the Hulks, especially those I interviewed, Oren Olson, Bob Montieth, Ed Phillips, and Roly Meunier.

The former Merchant Marine, US Army and US Navy Seamen who corresponded with me and gave me a glimpse into their experiences, Ian Ferguson of the SS Albertolite, Richard Powers of the SS Vitruvius, Andrew Bozard of the USAT L.J. Vicat, Jim Moore of the USAT Leonard Chase Wason, and John Partin of the USS Carmita.

Powell River artist Joanne Clark, for allowing me to use her charming painting, "The Hulks," on the cover.

Last, but not least, Robert Dufour, whose enthusiasm and expertise in layout and graphics finally brought this book to life.

The Hulks, from bottom: YOGN 82, Henri Le Chatelier, Quartz, P.M. Anderson, Peralta, Emile N. Vidal, John Smeaton, Thaddeus Merriman, L.J. Vicat and Armand Considere.

NorskeCanada Millennium Project

n 1930 the Powell River Company Limited took possession of the first of 19 ships' hulks to be used as floating breakwaters for the log pond at their pulp and paper mill at Powell River, British Columbia. Using decommissioned ship's hulls as breakwaters was not a new idea, or even very unusual — it had been done in many places along the West Coast, and around the world. However, in most cases ship breakwaters were created by sinking vessels in relatively shallow water, their upper hulls and superstructures remaining above the surface to break the waves. At Powell River the water is too deep to allow this, and the breakwater ships were kept afloat and ballasted to reduce the action of the sea. In fact the ships of the Powell River mill's Breakwater Fleet form what many believe to be the largest floating breakwater in the world. This book tells the story of this diverse group of ships, built from wood, steel and concrete, the Powell River landmark known as *The Hulks*.

1

A Breakwater of Ships

Hulk \n\ (from Middle English hulke, from Old English hulc, probably from Medieval Latin holcus, from Greek holkas, from helkein — to pull)

1 a: a heavy clumsy ship b: the body of an old ship unfit for service c: an abandoned wreck or shell d: a ship used as a prison

2 : one that is bulky or unwieldy

Webster's Dictionary

The province of British Columbia was built on the wealth of her natural resources — her fisheries, her minerals, her abundant sources of electrical power, and in particular, her forests. The granting of timber leases by the BC government around the turn of the century spurred the construction of a number of pulp, paper, and lumber mills along the coast. The subsequent wealth created by these operations made the forest industry the mainstay of the province's economy during the 20th Century.

The raw material for the production of pulp, paper, and lumber is, of course, logs. Harvested from the coastal forests of British Columbia, logs are transported to the mills in booms, in Davis rafts, and on barges towed by tugs. At the mills they are placed in log ponds and sorted as necessary according to species and size. Care must be taken that the logs don't remain in the water for too long as losses from sinking and damage from teredos (wood-boring worms) increase costs and reduce the profitability of a mill. An adequate quantity of logs must be kept on hand to ensure the continuous operation of mills during periods when deliveries of logs cannot be made due

The self-dumping log barge, Haida Carrier, dumps its load at a coastal mill.

NorskeCanada Millennium Project

to bad weather or supply problems. A mill's log pond must be large enough to store the logs, provide space for the unloading of barges, and allow the movement of booms and boats. It must also be protected from

Logs ride the log haul into the Powell River mill. In the background, Davis Rafts, barges and boomsticks provide a temporary breakwater.

NorskeCanada Millennium Project

wind and waves to prevent damage to booms, and to provide a safe work area for the people who work on and around them.

Several factors affected the choice of location for the pulp, paper, and lumber mill at Powell River, British Columbia, which started production in 1912.

The tug J.S. Foley tows a Davis Raft into the Powell River Company's Teakerne Arm booming ground.

Powell River Historical Museum

Powell Lake, which is directly behind the mill, offered plenty of power to generate electricity and run equipment. Stands of timber in the surrounding area were available for logging. The mill's location on the waterfront made delivery of logs by sea convenient and provided a good deep-water port to allow access for shipping. On the other hand, the open waterfront of the mill was exposed to some severe winds from the southeast, funnelling up Malaspina Strait, and from the northwest, blowing down from northern Vancouver Island. These winds could wreak havoc in the log pond, breaking up booms and making it an uncomfortable and hazardous place to work. Storms would occasionally result in the mill shutting down, the foul weather making it impossible to continue feeding logs to the mill.

The log pond was located south of the wharves that had been built during the construction of the mill, and this afforded some protection from northwest winds. Large boomsticks (logs that can be chained together) were moored to pilings and anchored offshore to help reduce the action of the waves. Log cribs, Davis rafts, and barges were also moored in front of the log pond as they waited to be unloaded or broken up. These served as temporary breakwaters. A small rock breakwater was built at the southern end of the log pond and a government wharf with floats for mooring small boats was erected, providing some shelter from southeasters. To ensure efficient inventory control and continuous operation of the mill, a one-month's supply of logs was considered

The train delivers a load of rock during construction of the rock breakwater in 1928.

NorskeCanada Millennium Project

necessary, and although these defences offered a relatively safe area to store the mill's logs, the log pond proved to be too small.

To help offset the lack of storage at the mill, the Powell River Company also ran log booming and storage areas at Squirrel Cove on Cortes Island, at Teakerne Arm on West Redonda Island, and at Scut-

(Top) Workmen prepare to set an anchor.

(Bottom) Divers maintain anchor chains for the Hulks.

NorskeCanada Millennium Project

tle Bay on the mainland a few miles north of the mill. The booming grounds provided protected areas where log barges could be unloaded and Davis rafts could be broken up. The logs could then be put into flat booms prior to being towed to the mill. These camps could provide an adequate supply of logs, but the cost of running and maintaining them was an added burden that company management would like to have eliminated. Operating log ponds at a distance from the mill created all kinds of inventory-control problems. Towing logs many miles after they had been stored for months resulted in losses due to logs sinking, and there was still the problem of getting the logs to the mill during periods of inclement weather.

As time passed several factors made expansion of the log pond crucial. Projects that had increased the production of the mill through the addition of paper machines and pulping equipment had been completed, and more were in the planning stages. Improvements in equipment and procedures made the mill more efficient and allowed faster throughput of logs, again increasing production. Finally, as the giant trees of the coast were logged off, the logs became smaller and more space was required in the log pond to store the same quantity of wood.

In 1928, to improve the log storage problem, a large rock breakwater was built to the south of the government wharf, more than doubling the size of the log pond. To build this breakwater, which would extend into deep water from the shore, the Powell River Company resurrected the Michigan & Puget Sound Railroad line. This logging railroad, which predated the mill, originally ran from Powell Lake, through Powell River Townsite to a log dump at Michigan Landing, known today as Willingdon Beach. The rail line now carried rock to the waterfront, blasted from a quarry alongside Powell River. Rails were laid on a trestle built out from shore and the rock was dumped from the rail cars to both sides. As the breakwater grew, more rails were added. Once the job had been completed, the rails were lifted and the rail line was permanently abandoned.

Rock breakwaters, while excellent for creating a wave barrier, are relatively expensive to build. The deep water in front of the mill would have made enclosing the log pond with rock extremely costly, and so the problem of how to protect the front of the log pond remained. It is not known whose inspiration resulted in the proposal to use ships as floating breakwaters. Perhaps someone noticed how well a loaded log barge, most of which were old ship's hulls, broke the waves when one was moored in front of the mill waiting to be unloaded. Wherever the idea came from, in 1930 the Powell River Company purchased the stripped hulls of two former U.S. Navy Cruisers and the history of The Hulks began.

Over the years 19 ship's hulks, built of steel, wood, or reinforced concrete have been brought to the mill with the intention of being used in the breakwater. Some of them only spent a few years on the breakwater line, while others stayed long enough to become local landmarks. In one notable case the ship was never used in the breakwater at all, and ended its days by being scuttled just offshore. The ten concrete ships that make up the breakwater today are all veterans; some have been in use for as long as 55 years.

Up to ten concrete anchors, each weighing between 14 and 16 tons, hold each of the hulks in place in water that ranges from 30 to 120 feet deep. The anchor chains are made up of 12-inch links and weigh about 55 pounds per foot. Bridle chains that connect the ships to each other also keep them an even distance apart. Severe storms can cause the anchors to

The bow of the concrete ship P.M. Anderson shows its age in this picture from the mossy afterdeck of the Quartz.

John A Campbell

drag and the ships must be repositioned occasionally. Wear and corrosion of the anchor and bridle chains is also a concern and regular inspection and maintenance is needed to reduce the risk of breakage. Divers are called on to inspect, repair, and replace worn sections as required. A 12-foot octopus had to be removed from an anchor during one repair so divers could connect the chains.

The Hulks are ballasted in order to increase their draft and improve their wave-breaking capability. Some of the older ships had gravel and log pond dredgings dumped into them as ballast. The concrete hulks, already heavier than steel ships of the same size, carry water ballast. To improve their ability to fend off the waves, the ships are heeled over slightly with their decks angled in towards shore. Occasionally, as accumulated rainwater and leakage offset the weight of the ballast, a ship will be seen to roll the other way, turning its bottom to the shore and facing its deck to the sea. Periodic inspection and pumping of the ships is necessary to keep them from sinking too low in the water.

The Hulks have been part of the scenery of Powell River for so long that, to residents, they seem to be a natural part of the waterfront. They are a favourite nesting and roosting spot for seabirds, and the water around them is a preferred haunt of seals, sea lions, and otters. Sport fishermen can be seen trolling near the old ships on most calm days. Local fishing reports testify to the area's productivity, with frequent tales of salmon caught near The Hulks.

The number and configuration of the ships in the breakwater has changed over the years, depending on the size of log pond required at any given time. The original development of the floating breakwater took place between 1928 and 1931 with the construction of the rock breakwater and the purchase of the first two hulks. The breakwater was reconfigured between 1945 and 1950 as the first two hulks were moved out farther into the strait and more steel and then concrete ships were added. In 1961 the breakwater was altered again, as all but one of the steel ships were removed and replaced with concrete hulks. Finally, in 1966 the remaining steel hulk was removed and a tenth concrete ship was added. The breakwater was "bellied" out into the strait as land in the log pond was reclaimed for the construction of a new sawmill.

The elements have taken a toll on the concrete ships over the years. Moss, grass, and small bushes have taken root on the decks. Deterioration of the concrete hulls has allowed water to reach some of the reinforcing steel, and rust has streaked the hulls over the remains of their blue-grey or olive green paint. Patches of concrete on the hulls have spalled off and exposed the first layer of reinforcing bar. By the 1990s, the wooden superstructures of the ships had deteriorated to the point that they had to be removed for safety reasons. Occasional collisions with logs, barges, and boats have also caused damage that required repairs.

Until recently there has always been a need for a large log pond and the existing ten ship breakwater has been necessary. However, downsizing of the mill has ended the use of raw logs at Powell River and the mill now relies on imported wood chips and purchased pulp to make its product. As a result, the future of the ship breakwater is becoming uncertain. Adding to the uncertainty is the deteriorating condition of the ships, which has caused concern about their ability to stay afloat. The possibility of the loss of one or more of the ships has led to projects to remove oil that was left aboard them from their active service days. This has minimised the potential for environmental damage in the event of a sinking.

In December 2002 another reconfiguration of the breakwater began. The ships were pulled in closer to shore, six of them arranged to form a protected moorage area for hog fuel and wood chip barges near the barge-offloading float. These six vessels have been selected to keep for the foreseeable future. The remaining four are considered to be surplus vessels. Three of them were anchored parallel to the shore to protect the waterfront and log dump near the rock breakwater. The last ship was left as an extension of the rock breakwater to take the brunt of the southeasters that gust up Malaspina Strait.

While the future of the floating breakwater has not been written, its past is documented in the following chapters — the intriguing histories of 19 ships that travelled the seas in many different occupations, but for a time found a place in Powell River's floating breakwater, known as The Hulks. ⚓

The Riverside neighborhood of Powell River, the mill and the Hulks in 1948.

NorskeCanada Millennium Project

2

The U.S. Cruisers

There is a homely adage which runs, 'Speak softly and carry a big stick; you will go far.' If the American nation will speak softly and yet build and keep at a pitch of the highest training a thoroughly efficient navy, the Monroe Doctrine will go far.

Theodore Roosevelt, Speech at the Minnesota State Fair, Sept. 2, 1901

A t 6:00 PM, October 25, 1930, the Kingcome Navigation tug, ST. FAITH arrived at Powell River with the first of two former United States Navy Cruisers to be placed in the breakwater. These ships were examples of the Pre-Dreadnought Era warship, holdovers from the days when naval battles were fought at relatively close range with batteries of both large and small calibre guns hurling destruction at the enemy. Once they were visually striking vessels, bristling with gun barrels and each with four vertical funnels, tall spotter's masts, and raked ram bows. The arrival of these former flagships of the American Asiatic Fleet marked the beginning of the floating ship breakwater at Powell River.

The tug St. Faith leaves Seattle Harbour with the hulk of the Charleston in tow.

Powell River Historical Museum

USS Charleston (C-22)

The first hulk to arrive was that of the USS CHARLESTON (C-22), a St. Louis class protected cruiser. Built by the Newport News Shipbuilding and Dry Dock Company of Newport News, Virginia, she was launched on January 23, 1904. The CHARLESTON, the third U.S. Navy vessel to bear this name, was commissioned on October 17, 1905 under the command of Captain H. Winslow.

USS CHARLESTON was 426.5 feet long, had a 66-foot beam, and a 22.5-foot draft. Normal displacement

was 9700 tons with a full load displacement of 10,839 tons. Sixteen Babcock and Wilcox boilers, operating at 250 pounds per square inch and producing 21,000 horsepower, drove her two vertical, 4-cylinder, triple expansion engines. She could attain a speed of 21.5 knots. Her bunkers could hold a full load of 1800 tons of coal. As many as 784 officers and men called the CHARLESTON home while at sea.

When she was commissioned the CHARLESTON's main battery consisted of fourteen 6-inch/50 calibre

The USS Charleston C-22 in 1908

US National Archives and Records Administration

With two triple expansion engines producing 21000 horsepower, the Charleston was capable of a speed of 21.5 knots.

US National Archives and Records Administration

rapid-fire guns. Her secondary battery was made up of eighteen 3-inch rapid-fire guns, twelve 3-pounder semi-automatic guns, eight one-pounder rapid-fire guns, and ten .30 calibre machine guns. Two 6-inch/50 calibre guns and fourteen 3-inch guns were removed during World War I, and two 3-inch/50 calibre anti-aircraft guns were added post-war.

One of the CHARLESTON's first duties after commissioning was to carry U.S. Secretary of State, Elihu Wood on goodwill visits to a number of South American ports during the summer of 1906. Having completed this diplomatic mission, the ship was moved to the Pacific Coast. There she served with the Pacific Squadron between the fall of 1906 and the summer of 1908.

In October 1908 the CHARLESTON was assigned to the Far East, where she served as the flagship of the Third Squadron of the Pacific Fleet, and later as the flagship of the Asiatic Fleet. The Asiatic fleet was based at Cavite in the Philippines during the winter, and moved north to Chefoo, China during the summer. It visited ports in China, Japan, Manchuria, and Russia, flying the American flag and serving as an example of Teddy Roosevelt's "Big Stick Diplomacy." The CHARLESTON returned to the West Coast, and was decommissioned at the Puget Sound Navy Yard in Bremerton, Washington in October 1910.

In September 1912 the CHARLESTON was recommissioned and assigned to the Pacific Reserve Fleet, serving as a receiving ship at the Puget Sound

Yard through the first part of 1916. In the spring of 1916 she was sent to the Canal Zone as a tender for U.S. submarines that were there on manoeuvres.

On April 6, 1917 the United States entered World War I. The CHARLESTON was returned to full commission and sent to the Caribbean to join the Patrol Force. Based in St. Thomas, Virgin Islands she patrolled for German raiders until the end of May, and then steamed to Philadelphia carrying U.S. Marines from Haiti. From Philadelphia the CHARLESTON escorted the first convoy carrying American troops to France, and arrived at the end of June. Once she had returned to New York, the CHARLESTON spent the rest of the war performing escort duties in the Atlantic between the Caribbean and Nova Scotia. In November 1918, with the signing of the Armistice, the ship joined the Cruiser and Transport Force and made five passages to France carrying occupation forces and returning with thousands of war veterans.

By August 1919, the CHARLESTON had returned to the West Coast and was placed in reduced commission at the Puget Sound Naval Yard. On July 17, 1920 the ship was reclassified from protected cruiser to cruiser and her number was changed from C-22 to CA-19 as part of the navy's reorganisation of the fleet. She was sent to San Diego, California that year, where she served as the administrative flagship for the

The Charleston (left) and the Huron, still fitted with her cage mast (right), at the scrapyard in 1930.

Courtesy of Frank A Clapp

commander of Destroyer Squadrons, Pacific Fleet. This was to be her final duty, and on June 4, 1923 she sailed north to Puget Sound where she was decommissioned in December.

The CHARLESTON remained in the Naval yard until February 1930, when she was sold to Abe Goldberg of Seattle for scrapping by the Lake Union Dry Dock and Machine Works. At the scrap-yard the ship was stripped of her superstructure, decks, equipment, and upper hull to her waterline. Relieved of the massive weight of the warship above, the lower hull floated high in the water. The Powell River Company purchased the hulk for $10,700 and paid $2159.68 to Canadian Customs for duty.

The much-heralded arrival of the CHARLESTON at Powell River was reported in the November 1930 issue of the Powell River Company's newsmagazine, The Digester. A section of the article "A Battleship for a Breakwater" reads:

A Disappointing Battleship

For weeks, the folk about here had been looking forward to the day "when the battleship should arrive." Many residents, more particularly among our romantic younger group, had visions of a trim, neat cruiser, her funnels rakishly set, her sharp bows cleaving the water in the wake of the (St.) Faith. They expected a battleship and pictured themselves playing tag on its immaculate decks, inspecting gun stations, and what not. There were some disappointed and surprised youngsters in Powell River when they caught their first glimpse of the "battleship.

Perhaps the most apt description of the old Charleston, as it stands now, is that of a gigantic, all steel Indian dugout canoe. With every ounce of metal removed, with only the shell of the lower hull remaining, she looks for all the world like an exaggerated edition of the large Indian dugouts which have not yet vanished from our coast.

The CHARLESTON was anchored off the end of the rock breakwater to protect the southern part of the log pond. Here the ship remained for 30 years, her long service a testament to her thick warship's hull

The hulk of the Charleston takes her place in the breakwater on a very calm October day in 1930.

which outlasted the hulls of many of the other steel breakwater ships. In 1945 the CHARLESTON was fitted with a windmill to power her bilge pump.

Even the thickest steel hull will rust through eventually, and three decades of exposure to salt water, wind, waves, and impacts from logs and boats took their toll on the old lady of the breakwater. As long time log pond employee Oren Olson recalled, "We could reach out with a pike pole and pull big sheets of rust off the steel hulks. We'd watch the rust sink, like leaves fluttering through the water."

By 1961 it was evident that the CHARLESTON would not be able to remain afloat for much longer, but much of her hull was still in reasonably good shape. Macmillan, Bloedel, and Powell River Limited, the new owners of the Powell River mill, made the decision to move her to their booming ground at Kelsey Bay on Vancouver Island, to continue her breakwater duties as a grounded hulk. Here the remains of the USS CHARLESTON can be seen today in the company of several other old ships' hulks.

USS Huron (CA-9)

At the end of August 1931 the stripped hulk of the USS HURON arrived at Powell River to join the CHARLESTON. The HURON was built by the Union Iron Works of San Francisco, California and was launched on July 21, 1904 as the USS SOUTH DAKOTA, Armoured Cruiser No. 9 (ACR-9). She was commissioned on January 27, 1908 with Captain James T. Smith in command.

At 504 feet long, with a beam of 70 feet and a draft of 26 feet, the SOUTH DAKOTA was the largest ship to join the breakwater. She had a normal displacement of 13,680 tons and a full load displacement of 15,138 tons. Like the CHARLESTON, she was fitted with 16 Babcock

and Wilcox boilers and two vertical, 4-cylinder, triple expansion engines. She produced 23,000 horsepower and could reach a speed of 22 knots. When fully loaded, her bunkers could hold 2233 tons of coal. About 890 officers and men sailed on the SOUTH DAKOTA.

In keeping with the style of naval armament of the day, the cruiser bristled with artillery. When commissioned, her main battery was made up of four 8-inch/45 calibre guns, two in a turret mounted on the forward deck and two in a similar turret on the aft deck. The SOUTH DAKOTA's secondary battery consisted of fourteen 6-inch/50 calibre breech loading rifles, eighteen 3-inch/50 calibre rapid-fire guns, and

(Top) The USS South Dakota ACR-9 before WW I, and (Bottom) after being fitted with a cage mast in 1909.

Courtesy of Joe Hartwell

twelve 3-pounder saluting guns. She was also fitted with two 18-inch submerged torpedo tubes. Eight 3-inch/50 calibre guns were removed during the First World War along with eight 3-pounder saluting guns. A pair of 3-inch anti-aircraft guns were added post war.

After commissioning, the SOUTH DAKOTA was assigned to the Armoured Cruiser Squadron of the U.S. Pacific Fleet and sailed off the West Coast of the United States until August, when she was sent on a cruise to Samoa. Returning in September 1908, she sailed off the Pacific coasts of Central and South America until mid-1909.

The SOUTH DAKOTA had been at sea for about 17 months, spending few days in port, and had cruised for about 30,000 miles when in August 1909 she went into the Hunter's Point yard in San Francisco harbour. Here she was to undergo a refit and overhaul in preparation for her next duty. While there she set a record for that port when 600 tons of barnacles were scraped from her bottom. The ship's entire bottom from stem to stern was fouled with a coating of sea life approximately two inches thick, some individual specimens measuring three inches in diameter. It was estimated that the growth weighed 25 pounds per square foot. The mass of growth was heavy enough to add 4½ inches to the draft of the huge vessel. One hundred and seventy-five men were employed for a full day to remove the layer of barnacles.

The SOUTH DAKOTA also had her foremast removed and replaced with a cage mast, a common feature of armoured cruisers and battleships of the era. The cage mast was designed to carry spotters aloft in the days when artillery fire was directed by eyesight. Its cage-like support structure could sustain multiple direct hits from enemy guns without collapsing. The only drawback to the cage mast was its flexibility, giving spotters a wild ride in heavy seas or during gun salvos.

After leaving San Francisco in the autumn of 1909, SOUTH DAKOTA rejoined the other seven vessels of the Armoured Cruiser Squadron and sailed westward. The squadron visited ports in the Admiralty Islands, the Philippines, China and Japan, and completed the cruise at Honolulu in January 1910.

In February, the SOUTH DAKOTA and the USS TENNESSEE (ACR-10) formed a Special Service Squadron which sailed off the Atlantic Coast of South America until the end of the year, when they returned to the Pacific. The SOUTH DAKOTA sailed the Pacific Coast for most of 1911 and then rejoined the Armoured Cruiser Squadron in December for another Pacific cruise. This trip took her to ports in the Hawaiian Islands, the Marianas, the Philippines, and Japan. Returning to the American West Coast in August 1912, the SOUTH DAKOTA took part in squadron exercises until she was placed in reserve on December 1913 at the Puget Sound Navy Yard. SOUTH DAKOTA spent the next three years in and out of reserve, during which time she was sent on several cruises and put back in reserve on her return to Puget Sound. From September 1915 until February 1916 she served as the flagship of the Pacific Fleet Reserve Force.

On April 6, 1917 the United States entered World War I and the

The hulk of the Charleston, in the foreground, is stripped to the waterline.
The Huron undergoes scrapping in the background.

Powell River Historical Museum

SOUTH DAKOTA was returned to full commission. She was transferred to the Atlantic and joined Armoured Cruisers USS PITTSBURG (ACR-4), USS FREDERICK (ACR-8), and USS PUEBLO (ACR-7), patrolling the South Atlantic Ocean from Brazilian ports. In November 1918 she escorted troop convoys from the eastern U.S. to the mid-Atlantic, where British Cruisers took over. After the Armistice was signed, the SOUTH DAKOTA made two passages from France to New York, bringing American troops home.

The hulks of the Charleston (left) and the Huron (right) in their original positions in the breakwater.

NorskeCanada Millennium Project

In the summer of 1919 the SOUTH DAKOTA was reassigned to the Pacific to serve as the flagship of the Asiatic Fleet. She spent the following seven years in this duty, sailing out of the Philippines in the winter and out of Shanghai and Chefoo, China in the summer. On June 7, 1920 the SOUTH DAKOTA was renamed USS HURON, leaving her former name available for use by a new battleship. On July 17 she was reclassified from armoured cruiser to cruiser and her number was changed from ACR-9 to CA-9.

On the last day of 1926 the HURON sailed for home, arriving at the Puget Sound Navy Yard in March. She was decommissioned in June 1927 and placed in reserve until November 1929, when she was struck from the Navy lists. The HURON was sold for scrap in February 1930 in compliance with the London Treaty for the Limitation and Reduction of Naval Armament.

The HURON entered the Lake Union Dry Dock and Machine Works scrap-yard just behind the CHARLESTON and work was begun on her after scrapping of the other cruiser was completed. Like the CHARLESTON, she was stripped to her waterline leaving her canoe-like lower hull floating high in the water. In 1931 the Powell River Company purchased the hulk for $11,600 and paid $2,343.75 to Canadian Customs for duty.

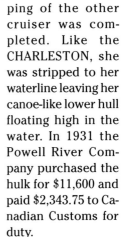

Upon her arrival at Powell River in late August 1931, under tow of the tug, ROOSEVELT, the HURON was anchored off the stern of the hulk of the CHARLESTON. Here she remained for almost 30 years, rusting away peacefully, and providing protection from the strong southeasters that rolled up the strait. In 1945, like her sister the CHARLESTON, she was fitted with a windmill-powered bilge pump that helped to keep the large open hull free of water.

Normal maintenance of the steel breakwater hulks included pumping out the hulls regularly to remove rainwater and seawater that leaked in over time. As water built up in the hulls, the ships would sit lower and lower in the water. On February 18, 1961 with a storm raging and the HURON in need of pumping, the once proud ship lost her battle with her enemy of 30 years and slipped quietly beneath the waves. She settled to the bottom of the log pond in about 80 feet of water and rests there to this day. ⚓

3

The First World War
Wooden Freighter

Although the wood ships never could compete with fast steel cargo carriers in the Trans-Atlantic trade, they made more than enough voyages to convince us that our policy in building them was not mistaken. They should have been regarded as a legitimate war expense, junked off and charged off, just as the Army sold millions of dollars of war supplies at any price and junked and charged off hundreds of miles of military railway track laid in France for the supply of our troops.

Edward N. Hurley, Chairman of the United States Shipping Board
The Bridge to France, 1927

owell River's government wharf was the town's link to the outside world during the 1930s. Projecting into the log pond between the mill's wharves and the rock breakwater, it served as a terminal for the passenger and freight steamships that served the British Columbia coast. The Imperial Oil Company had offices at the wharf and floats for small boat moorage were provided on its north side. Local logging companies also used the wharf, and a log dump was built near the end. Trucks could discharge their loads of logs, pulp blocks and shingle bolts

seven million gross tons of shipping by the warring nations, and the diversion of much of the huge British merchant fleet to the war effort prompted the U.S. Congress to pass a bill allowing the formation of the United States Shipping Board. The board was formed with the purpose of developing a Merchant Marine and Naval Reserve to meet the needs of the country's commerce. It was given the authority to build and acquire vessels, and to form corporations as needed to meet this end. The powers granted to the USSB gave them complete control over American ships and shipping.

Wooden-hulled ships for the Emergency Fleet Corporation under construction at the Gray's Harbor Yards, Aberdeen, Washington in 1919.

US National Archives and Records Administration

directly into the south log pond. The Powell River Company granted the logging companies the use of the south log pond for booming and shipment of their products.

While the rock breakwater and the hulks of the two cruisers provided protection for the south log pond, the log dump at the government wharf could be exposed to severe wave action during southeast winds. To help protect this area, the first wooden hulk was brought to Powell River. It was a type of ship that was built by the hundreds toward the end of the First World War. Few of these vessels ever saw any service and the wooden freighters of World War I were considered to be one of the more blatant examples of wartime wastefulness.

At the beginning of World War I, the United States was heavily dependent upon foreign merchant fleets for the shipping of her trade goods. At that time only about ten per cent of America's waterborne commerce, as measured in dollars, was being transported in American flag vessels. The sudden withdrawal of

The unprecedented number of ships that were being sunk by German U-boats lent urgency to the work of the USSB, especially after Germany announced its intention to adopt a policy of indiscriminate sinking of merchant vessels. The allies of the U.S. had appealed for "ships, ships, and more ships," and this appeal was to be met with the formation of the Emergency Fleet Corporation shortly after the U.S. declared war. The declaration of war transformed the USSB from a civilian agency to a military one with the sole purpose of bridging the Atlantic with ships and allowing the continued flow of men and material to Europe. The Emergency Fleet Corporation was given sweeping powers, and they took over the management of existing ships and shipyards and built many more.

The Emergency Fleet Corporation granted contracts for the building of five different classes of ships. These were: wood ships; fabricated steel ships (built from components made in shops, which were brought to the shipyard for assembly); composite ships (built from a combination of steel and wood components); concrete ships; and conventional ships of the pre-war type.

The wooden shipbuilding program was met with some controversy as many thought that the construction of wooden vessels would be a waste of money and resources. Wooden freight ships could not compete with the faster and more efficient steel ships of the time, and therefore would be of no use after the war was over. However, the abundance of wood that was available and the feeling that steel production

A typical USSB Emergency Fleet Corporation wooden freighter painted in wartime "dazzle paint."

US National Archives and Records Administration

would have difficulty meeting the demands of the entire shipbuilding program outweighed these concerns. The Emergency Fleet Corporation originally planned to award contracts to build 1017 wood ships for its program. Of these, 703 contracts were actually awarded, but when the Armistice was signed in November 1918 many contracts were cancelled. Some of the ships still under construction were completed, and a total of 589 freighters were built. However, only 118 ships were actually delivered to the Emergency Fleet Corporation and of those only 87 were in service for more than one month. The other 502 ships saw no service whatsoever and were eventually sold, scrapped, or scuttled.

On the Pacific Coast, 24 shipyards in the states of Oregon and Washington were put to work building wooden freighters for the war effort, launching a total of 220 ships. These ships were the work of Theodore E. Ferris, a prominent eastern naval architect who was responsible for designing the majority of the Emergency Fleet Corporation's vessels. His work was so recognisable at the time that it was common to refer to Emergency Fleet Corporation ships, whether of steel, wood, or concrete, as "Ferris ships." After the end of the war, Seattle's Lake Union was left

with a "mothball fleet" of about 38 of these freighters in different stages of completion. Eleven of these vessels ended up in British Columbia waters, most of them to be used as BC's first fleet of log barges.

The Blatchford

On June 6, 1919 the BLANDFORD, Emergency Fleet Corporation contract #98 was launched. Built by Sanderson & Porter Company of Raymond, Washington to Ferris's design, she was delivered on June 30 as an undocumented vessel. The BLANDFORD was typical of the wooden Ferris ships. Her length was 281 feet overall, she had a beam of 46 feet, a depth of 23.8 feet, and was of 2250 gross tons. The design called for the installation of a pair of coal-fired watertube boilers to power a triple expansion engine of 1400 horsepower. However, as the ship was destined to become one of the many surplus vessels left over from the First World War shipbuilding program, no equipment was installed.

The BLANDFORD joined the line of unneeded hulls in Lake Union, which was nicknamed "Wilson's Wood Row" after wartime President Woodrow Wilson. Here

FLOATING ELEVATOR NOW READY FOR SERVICE IN RELIEVING GRAIN-LOADING CONGESTION IN HARBOR

The Blatchford undergoes conversion to a floating grain elevator/lighter in Vancouver, 1924.

Photo from Vancouver Daily Province, courtesy of Frank A Clapp

she remained until March 1924 when she was purchased and towed to Vancouver. She became the first
Emergency Fleet Corporation hull to come to British
Columbia, and avoided the fate of most of her sisters, which were burned for their scrap metal.

The BLANDFORD was towed to False Creek in Vancouver and was renamed BLATCHFORD, after
Kenneth Blatchford, the mayor of Edmonton, Alberta.
Mr. Blatchford was also vice president of the British
Oriental Elevator and Grain Company Ltd., a company that had leased the Woodward Elevator from
the Vancouver Harbour Board. This company, in an-
ticipation of large overseas grain shipments, had decided to use a "lighter system" to transport grain to
ships in the harbour. Used successfully in many ports,
this type of operation made it unnecessary for ships
to dock under the spouts at the grain elevators. Instead the grain would be loaded onto the lighters,
which were then towed out to the ships at anchor.
There the grain was transferred to the ships. This
system reduced the time spent by ships waiting to
get to the elevators, and thereby reduced congestion
in the harbour.

Work was commenced by the Pacific Construction
Company to convert the BLATCHFORD for this duty.
The hull had three large holds, which had a capacity
of approximately 75,000 bushels of grain. Two con-

*The log barge Abnoba, a former USSB wooden freighter
hull, with a load of logs off Powell River. Her windmill
powered a bilge pump.*

NorskeCanada Millennium Project

veyors ran the length of the hull and an elevator tower
was built at the forward end to allow the grain to be
lifted and spouted into the holds of the grain ships.
The lighter was also equipped to handle grain in
sacks. It was expected that this floating grain elevator would be able to transfer her full load in five
hours.

By the time that work was completed on the
BLATCHFORD, the large grain shipments for which
she had been converted were already past and congestion in the harbour was no longer a problem.
Never to be used for grain handling, the ship remained

*This out of focus picture of a warship passing the log pond is one of the few
to show the Blatchford in use as a breakwater ship.*

Powell River Historical Museum

in False Creek for more than four years. Finally, in January 1928 the BLATCHFORD became the property of the Vancouver Harbour Commission. She was raised from the mud of False Creek, where she had settled after being sunk to swell her seams. She had her elevator tower removed and was moved to Bedwell Bay for storage.

In November 1928 the A.P. Allison Logging Company acquired the BLATCHFORD and converted her into a log barge. She joined several of her USSB sisters, which were already being used in this capacity. The use of ships' hulls as log barges was a welcome advance in the transport of logs on the BC coast. With the ability to move logs in all but the worst weather, with no losses from broken booms, sinkage, or damage from teredos, and at a higher speed than possible with the Davis raft, the companies enjoyed lower insurance rates and lower operating costs.

Each log barge was manned by a crew of between three and eight men, under the command of a barge master. The crew was responsible for the loading and unloading of the barge, and steered the barge when under tow. An engineer and fireman operated the boiler and winches on barges that carried loading equipment.

Log barges received hard use. The handling of the huge logs found in BC in those days was a tricky business, and losing control of one of the forest giants could cause considerable damage. Shifting loads during rough weather was another danger and sprung planks or broken framework were not uncommon. Navigating the coastal waters of BC presented many challenges as well, and several barges were stranded or sunk. As the wood-hulled barges were lost or damaged beyond use, steel-hulled barges replaced them.

On January 31, 1934 the BLATCHFORD's certificate was cancelled and her name was removed from the registry after her owner advised the authorities that the barge was a derelict. Sometime in 1936 she was towed to Powell River where the hulk was moored south of the government wharf. Here, in company with the CHARLESTON and the HURON, she protected the log dump at the end of the wharf and the booming ground to the south from the wind and waves.

By 1939 the BLATCHFORD had sunk, gradually settling into the sludge on the bottom of the log pond.

The bow of the Blatchford in the log pond after sinking in 1939.

Powell River Historical Museum

Although her hull was underwater, her bow still protruded above the surface and she presented a hazard to tugs and boats that used the government wharf. In March 1945, an attempt was made to break the hulk up by blasting. This proved to be less than effective. Powell River Company communications from November of the same year mention problems that were encountered in trying to remove the old BLATCHFORD from her resting-place on the bottom. This is the last mention of the former USSB ship. It must be assumed that she was eventually broken up, and that if anything remains of her it will be found on the bottom near the place of her sinking. ⚓

In 1945, the Blatchford was broken up by blasting.

Powell River Historical Museum

4

The Windjammers

The windjammers... tall ships from around the world whose very presence bespeaks man's centuries-old struggle against the inexorabilities of the sea.

Deirdre Carmody, June 1986

n the early 1940s, with World War II raging overseas, the Powell River Company was occupied with wartime production concerns: operating an assembly plant for the Boeing Aircraft Company on their mill site as well as pulp, paper, and lumber manufacturing. But behind the scenes a strategy for post-war expansion and modernisation of the mill was being developed. As part of these plans, enlargement of the mill's log storage area was under consideration. Many options were contemplated, including building a storage area at the mouth of Powell River, the construction of a log pond to the south of the rock breakwater, and the enlargement of the existing log pond with pilings and extension of the rock breakwater. All of these ideas were rejected as being impractical or too expensive.

The CHARLESTON and HURON had proven their worth over 15 years of service and it was decided that the most cost-effective solution to the log storage problem would be to obtain more ship's hulks

and to extend the floating breakwater. In late 1945, with the war over, the company's managers began a search for suitable hulks.

The war had been over for only a few months, so surplus vessels were not yet readily available. Several ships that had been damaged by grounding or by fire were considered, but they proved to be unsuitable. Finally, in November 1945, two vessels were located. Both had been in use on the coast as barges for many years, but they had histories that hearkened back to the last days of commercial sailing vessels on the world's oceans.

The Malahat

The auxiliary schooner MALAHAT was, undoubtedly, the most colourful and notorious of British Columbia's ships, and she was considered by many who sailed on her to be the luckiest. While she never formed a part of the breakwater, she was acquired by

The five-masted auxiliary schooner Malahat anchored at an Australian Port.

La Trobe Picture Collection, State Library of Victoria, Australia the company for that purpose and deserves mention in this book.

The MALAHAT was one of 19 "Mabel Brown" class 5-masted wooden schooners that were built in British Columbia shipyards during the First World War. BC lumber producers were desperate for a method of transporting their product to markets after the withdrawal of merchant shipping for the war effort. While lumber producers in the United States had operated their own fleet of lumber carriers for years, those in Canada had relied on regular merchant ships. In 1916 the sawmill owners collectively and successfully lobbied the British Columbia government for financial support to build their own fleet of ships.

Cameron-Genoa Mills Shipbuilding Limited of Victoria, BC built six of the "Mabel Brown" class ships, including the MALAHAT. At 245 feet in length and with a 43-foot beam, the MALAHAT was capable of carrying as much as 1.8 million board feet of lumber, including a ten-foot high deck load, or a large load of general cargo.

The schooners were rigged "bald headed," that is, with no topsails. The mainsails were set from deck using steam-powered winches. Both of these factors reduced the number of crew required to sail the ships. This was an important consideration as the days of the sailing ship were nearly done and experienced tall-ship sailors were becoming scarce. The MALAHAT was also equipped with a pair of Swedish "Bolinder" 160 horsepower, 2-cycle semi-diesel engines, a cantankerous breed of machine that carried torches mounted on the cylinder heads to provide heat for ignition until they were thoroughly warmed up. While the MALAHAT was considered to be at her best under sail, these engines gave her the ability to carry on, albeit slowly, when the winds died.

The MALAHAT's crew was housed in the forecastle of the ship, while the officers had rather luxurious quarters aft. The owner's stateroom, heated with a coal-burning fireplace, was also equipped with a full-sized bathtub. The captain's stateroom and the stateroom for the mates, engineer and cook were also heated, and a second full-sized bathtub was shared between them.

The MALAHAT was launched in Victoria on August 11, 1917 without ceremony, and was immediately pressed into service. Although her engines had not been installed, she was loaded with laths and lumber in Victoria and was then towed to Port Alberni where she was loaded with 1.5 million board feet of timber. Fully loaded, her sails were raised and she began her first voyage, arriving in Sydney, Australia

66 days later. On her return trip the schooner carried a cargo of lard, 1500 tons of copra, 250,000 board feet of Australian hardwood lumber, and five bales of horns and hooves for making glue. This load was dropped off in Seattle and the MALAHAT returned to Victoria where her engines and tanks were installed.

The schooner carried many different cargoes during her life as a merchant sailing ship. Lumber, from Canadian and American coastal mills, was shipped to Australia; coal was carried from Australia to Peru and loads of nitrates were carried as far away as England. John Archibald Campbell, who served on the MALAHAT's first voyage as second mate and on her second voyage as first mate cargo, left this record of the ship's travels:

> Carried lumber to Inquique, Chile, there to Hilo with nitrate, to San Francisco light. Loaded with gasoline for Japan and from Japan light to Columbia River, a record crossing of twenty days. To Port Perry, Australia with lumber, from Australia with wheat to Callao, Peru. Down the coast to Taltal, Chile and picked up a load of nitrate for Honolulu in 1918. Honolulu back to Columbia River where I left the ship.

Although she was built during wartime, the MALAHAT's only contact with the war came in 1917 while in harbour in Inquique, Chile. Of the 20 ships in port, 18 were German ships that had been interred by the Chilean government. While they were technically under arrest, Chile had few soldiers available, and groups of armed German sailors roamed the town with impunity, harassing the crews of the few allied vessels. One night, while at anchor in the crowded harbour, an alert watchman noticed a pair of rowboats stealthily making their way towards the MALAHAT's anchor cables. When he raised the alarm the ship's crew crowded onto the deck and the Germans were scared off, disappearing among the many anchored vessels.

The conclusion of the First World War spelled the end for many commercial sailing ships, which were unable to compete with the steamships released from their wartime duties. However the MALAHAT, with her customary good fortune, was saved by the enactment of the Volstead Act in 1920 and the beginning of Prohibition in the United States. During Prohibition the smuggling of alcohol to thirsty Americans became a lucrative business in British Columbia for those willing to brave the seas and possible capture by the U.S. Coast Guard.

The MALAHAT was to become legendary as the Queen of Rum Row, mother ship to the rum fleet. Loaded with 60,000 cases of liquor, she would sail outside the territorial waters of the United States to avoid arrest by the Coast Guard and take up station in "Rum Row," directed by wireless radio transmissions from her owners in Vancouver. The exact location of Rum Row changed depending on circumstances. It could be off the California coast outside the twelve-mile limit or off Mexico just south of the American border. Fast "Mosquito" boats would swarm out to meet the MALAHAT, load with liquor and race to shore, hopefully without running into the law.

To make handling of the liquor easier, the bottles were removed from their cases and sewn, 12 at a time, into burlap sacks. This is believed to be the origin of the West Coast slang term, a "sack of beer;"

broken. Crewmen were stationed atop the ship's masts to watch for the American Coast Guard cutters.

On one occasion, while being shadowed by a particularly persistent Coast Guard vessel, the captain ordered that sacks filled with sand be lowered overboard and be marked with a buoy. While the American boat was busy trying to recover what was believed to be a cache of liquor, the schooner slipped quietly away to her next rendezvous point.

Another time, under the cover of night, floats with torches set in the same configuration as the MALAHAT's lights were set up, the schooner's lights were extinguished and she sailed off. When dawn arrived the big ship appeared to have vanished, much to the Coast Guard captain's consternation.

Pressure from the Americans finally resulted in the revocation of the MALAHAT's radio licence by the

The Malahat, the world's first self-propelled, self-loading log barge, with a deck load of logs.

Vancouver Maritime Museum

used when referring to a case of beer, a "half sack" being a six-pack.

While many of her sister rum runners were arrested by the U.S. Coast Guard, skilful navigation by her captains and a considerable amount of trickery allowed the MALAHAT to avoid this fate. As long as she stayed outside of American waters, no laws were

Canadian government. The rum runner's response was to hire an electronics wizard who designed a radio set that could be easily hidden and didn't require a fixed aerial.

As a sailing ship, the MALAHAT had an advantage over the occasional over-zealous Coast Guard officer. If the lookouts spotted a cutter that looked intent on boarding the schooner outside of U.S. territorial waters, the ship's sails were raised and she would be sailed straight out to sea. The Coast Guard could follow only at the risk of running out of fuel.

The authorities were not the only threat to the rumrunners. Hijackings by the criminal element were also a real danger and precautions were taken to protect the cargo and crews. Weapons were in plain view on deck during the transfer of liquor to boats. The crews of boats being loaded from the MALAHAT were not usually permitted to board the schooner. A ladder and a small landing were lowered from which the rumrunners could do business. Payment was passed to the MALAHAT's master and the cargo and receipt was hoisted down into the waiting boats under the watchful eyes of the MALAHAT's shotgun toting deckhands.

By 1933 it was apparent that "the great social and economic experiment" that was prohibition had failed miserably and was about to be repealed. With alcohol available in the United States legally, the glory days of the rumrunners were over. The MALAHAT was withdrawn from Rum Row and was sold in 1934.

For a short period of time the MALAHAT returned to her original occupation as a lumber carrier, but with disastrous results. The company that had purchased the schooner intended to use her to carry logs from the Prince Rupert area, but the inexperience of her captain and crew at handling the great weight of the logs made this enterprise less than successful. Finally, after picking up a load of aspen logs at Prince Rupert, the schooner went aground on a reef near the Holland Rock lighthouse. She was lightened by removing her cargo and was refloated on the high tide the next morning. The MALAHAT limped back to Vancouver with no logs in her hold and was placed under arrest by Deputy Marshall W.B. Cochrane for unpaid wages and repair bills totalling $3800. Under an Admiralty Court order, the MALAHAT was put up for sale for $2500, although she had cost $750,000 to build.

The schooner was something of a white elephant even at this bargain price. She was far too big to be used as a yacht and needed a crew of 15 to 20 men to sail her. She was too slow to be profitable as a cargo vessel. For some time it seemed as if the ship would lie at her moorings until she was scrapped, but her luck had not run out yet.

The Gibson Brothers, well known West Coast loggers, had been looking for a source of spare parts for the Bolinder engines in their boat, OTTER. The engines were uncommon on this coast and the Gibsons were aware that the MALAHAT was fitted with these same engines and carried many spare parts in her engine room. When they heard that the schooner had

The Malahat, under tow of the tug, James Carruthers, operated as a towed barge after her engines were removed.

Courtesy of Council of Marine Carriers

been seized and was for sale, they visited the lawyer in charge and offered to buy the parts. They were informed that the ship had to be sold intact and that the first certified cheque for $2500 would buy her. The Gibsons made a snap decision and bought the MALAHAT sight unseen.

When they went to inspect their purchase the brothers were stunned by their good fortune. In addition to $1500 worth of spare engine parts that she carried, the MALAHAT's tanks were full of oil worth $1000, her canvas could be sold for $1000, and her two anchor chains were worth between $2000 and $3000 each.

The only problem remaining was what to do with the ship. In 1935 the Gibsons met Tom Kelley, a logger who was contracted to the Powell River Company to supply the mill with logs from the Queen Charlotte Islands. Kelley transported his logs in Davis rafts during the summer, but couldn't move any logs for five months during the winter. Losses from foul weather made insurance costs intolerable, and logs stored in the Queen Charlotte Islands over the winter were exposed to teredo damage.

With the MALAHAT lying idle and building up moorage and watchman's fees, the Gibsons needed to put the ship to work. They proposed to Kelley that they would sail the schooner to the Queen Charlottes, load up with spruce logs and deliver them to the Powell River Company's booming ground at Teakerne Arm for a cost of five dollars per thousand feet. Kelley agreed and the Gibsons began the process of converting the MALAHAT into what Gordon Gibson claimed was the world's first self-propelled, self-loading and unloading log barge.

A crew — consisting of a combination of sailors, loggers, and longshoremen — was assembled under the command of Captain John Vosper, one of the ship's masters during her rum running days. Two steam donkey engines were purchased to lift and swing the huge logs into place. The ship would carry a large deck load as well as having her hold full, so a raised bridge was constructed to allow the helmsman to see over the top of the logs.

On November 25, 1935 the MALAHAT motored out of Vancouver harbour headed for Nanaimo to load coal for her boiler, beginning the first of many hair-raising adventures under the ownership of the Gibsons. As they sailed north from Vancouver Island a storm blew up. In the gale, which was blowing be-

tween 50 and 60 knots, and with poor visibility, the Gibsons and the captain became unsure of the ship's position. The crew, miserably seasick and inexperienced, could not take down the sails in the heavy weather. In desperation they dropped both anchors and swung the schooner around into the wind. As the MALAHAT came about, the howling wind blew out every sail, the canvas shredding with a sound like cannons firing. The schooner never voyaged under sail again, as the Gibsons didn't have the funds to replace the tattered canvas or the skills to repair it.

The MALAHAT's life with the Gibson Brothers was a hard one. On her first trip to the Queen Charlottes her holds were enlarged to 50 feet in length by removing beams and opening up her decks. One of her masts was removed to allow the huge logs to be swung aboard. Gibson's on-the-spot modifications to the ship nearly caused a mutiny by the captain and part of the crew, as they became concerned about the integrity of her structure. The loading and transport of the massive logs also caused much damage to the ship, especially when the logs shifted or broke

The Malahat, moored to the Huron, lies awash in the Powell River log pond. A group of Powell River Company managers assess the hulk's condition from the poop deck..

NorskeCanada Millennium Project

loose in rough weather. On more than one occasion the MALAHAT's planks and framing were sprung open, only to be pulled back together and patched by the Gibsons' crew using cables, logs and plywood.

The Gibson Brothers were experienced West Coast mariners, but none of them had captain's papers, a fact that made operation of the MALAHAT problematic at times. Qualified captains would look the ship over and refuse to go to sea in her. Captain Vosper never sailed on the ship after her first voyage to the Queen Charlotte Islands, objecting strongly to having his ship cut up under him. Once, after another captain had turned down a berth on the vessel, Gordon Gibson invited him below for a hot rum. When he came topsides after several drinks he found that the ship had sailed and that he had been "Shanghaied."

The beat-up condition of the schooner prompted the government to order the MALAHAT arrested, but for some time the Gibsons managed to stay one step ahead of the authorities. Finally the government ship, ADVERSUS caught up with them at Alert Bay and the MALAHAT was ordered to "stand by in the name of the King." Gordon Gibson was charged with operating a ship after it had been condemned and operating a ship without a master. The charges were eventually dismissed, but he was ordered to make repairs to the ship and not to make any more trips without a qualified captain aboard.

The former rumrunner carried her cargoes of logs to booming grounds and log ponds all over the British Columbia coast until 1937 when she limped into Bamfield harbour on one engine, having broken the tailshaft on the other. This was the end of her life as a powered vessel. The Gibsons had her engines and remaining masts removed and her hulk was used for the rest of her career as a towed log barge. She delivered her cargoes around the coast until March

A propeller shaft skeg on the wreck of the Malahat.

Courtesy of Jacques Marc

1944 when she was caught in a gale off the west coast of Vancouver Island and broke away from her tug. With the load of logs broken loose inside the hold, her hull was pounded, opening up her seams. The barge filled with water and only her cargo kept her afloat.

The MALAHAT was recovered later and towed into Uchucklesit Inlet where she lay for more than a year, eventually breaking loose from her moorings. The Department of Transport finally declared her a hazard to navigation and the Gibsons were ordered in October 1945 to remove her promptly.

During the same time at Powell River, the hulks of the CHARLESTON and the HURON had been moved seaward from their original positions in the log pond. This increased the area of the south log pond and also created a gap between the rock breakwater and the CHARLESTON. The managers of the Powell River Company were looking for a suitable hulk to fill this gap. At the same time the Gibsons were looking for some way to dispose of the battered MALAHAT. The loggers put a load of logs aboard the barge, as necessary to keep the old ship afloat as to make the tow worthwhile, and she began her last voyage.

The MALAHAT arrived at Powell River at about 12:30 PM on November 9, 1945. As Oren Olson recalled, "We had to unload the logs with the company pile driver because she had no steam on her." Unloaded and moored to the hulk of the HURON, the MALAHAT sat with her decks awash while management at the mill tried to decide what to do with her.

Head office in Vancouver seemed convinced that the old schooner would be ideal to protect the gap at the rock breakwater, but the people at Powell River could see from her condition that placing her in the gap, laid broadside to any southeaster that blew up would probably result in her breaking up. Consideration was given to using the barge to extend the line formed by the CHARLESTON and HURON. This idea was dropped because of the fear that if the MALAHAT sank, which was highly likely in her condition, she could drift around causing an underwater hazard in the log pond like the BLATCHFORD. A suggestion that the MALAHAT be used at the booming ground at Scuttle Bay was not pursued because she was floating so low in the water that it would have been impossible to tow her into the shallow bay. A proposal to offer the hulk for use at the new government wharf at Westview was also scrapped.

Finally, on November 26, a tremendous storm sealed the MALAHAT's fate. High winds and waves, combined with a high tide, caused havoc in the log pond. The old schooner broke loose from her moorings; the cables holding her had pulled the mooring points right out of the wooden hull. The tugs, TEESHOE and MACKENZIE were sent out to tow her back into position and secure her. This storm proved that to use the MALAHAT anywhere around the log pond would be inviting disaster.

She lay at her moorings in the log pond until the following July. By this time, her hull was so waterlogged that she was starting to drag down the other hulks that she was moored to. The decision was finally made to scuttle the old ship.

"I helped sink the MALAHAT," Oren Olsen remembered. "We put a charge in her and towed her outside the log pond by the rock breakwater. It was just after lunch when it was set off. Everyone thought that she would go straight down, but she didn't sink until the next morning."

Today the wreck of the MALAHAT is a popular sport diving site. Her bow lies in shallow water and her stern is about 80 feet deep at high tide. The ship settled to bottom upside down, but over the years has collapsed with her keel to starboard and her frames extending to port. Her tanks, hawse pipes, and propeller skegs are all that remain of her metal components.

The name of the wreck that lies just south of the breakwater was undocumented for many years, and while local old-timers knew the ship as the MALAHAT, no evidence other than memories could confirm this. Documents and photographs that turned up in the old Powell River Company records during the research for this book have finally confirmed the identity of the wreck and the reason that she was brought to Powell River.

The Island Carrier

The second barge that was purchased actually took a place in the breakwater for a period of time. The ISLAND CARRIER, a steel-hulled hog fuel barge owned by Island Tug and Barge Limited of Victoria, was the only vessel to leave the breakwater and continue with a career on the sea. Though she performed her rather unglamorous duties as a towed barge on the British

The four-masted steel barque Somali, the largest sailing vessel in the British Merchant Fleet

La Trobe Picture Collection, State Library of Victoria, Australia

Columbia coast for many years, she had been launched in 1892 as the huge 4-masted barque SOMALI, the largest sailing vessel in the British merchant fleet.

Russell and Company built the SOMALI at Port Glasgow, Scotland for the Hillsboro Ship Company, managed by Gilbert M. Steeves and Company of Liverpool. She was launched in August 1892, an enormous steel-hulled ship, 329 feet, 9 inches in length, with a 47 foot beam, 27 feet deep, and of 3537 gross tons. She was rigged as a 4-masted barque, her three forward masts carrying square sails and her mizzenmast

The Island Carrier in the breakwater with the mill in the background.

NorskeCanada Millennium Project

rigged fore and aft for ease of handling and manoeuvrability.

Unlike the speedy clipper ships of earlier times that relied on fast passages carrying relatively small cargoes to pay their way, the big merchant ships of the late 1800s made up for their slightly slower passages by filling their cavernous holds with great amounts of bulk and general cargo. The SOMALI was the height of this type of ship design, few others being able to match her capacity as she sailed to distant ports all around the world.

Master Mariner Captain Daniel J. MacDonald recalled when he shipped out on the SOMALI as a young bosun, bound for Calcutta carrying general cargo. The ship had an uneventful voyage to India, but the return trip to England took a tragic turn. As the ship rounded the Cape of Good Hope the captain became ill and died. The chief officer took command of the ship but also died, followed soon after by the second officer. The crew assumed that the ship's officers had died of the plague, and that they had escaped infection as their lodgings were well separated from the officer's quarters in the stern. Once the second officer had been buried at sea none of the crew entered the officer's cabin again.

The tragedy left the ship and its 24 crewmen without any officers to navigate her back to England. Two options were available to the crew. They could head for the nearest port and wait for officers to be sent from England, which could take months; or they could attempt to complete the voyage themselves, without officers aboard. The crew voted on the problem and the majority chose the latter alternative. Young MacDonald, who was studying for his Board of Trade navigation papers, was elected to command the ship. Twice on the trip up the African coast members of the crew agitated to put into port, but the majority of the crew voted to carry on. Finally, 32 days after the second officer had been buried at sea the SOMALI reached England.

The SOMALI sailed under the British flag until 1900 when she was sold to Aktiengesellschaft Alster of Hamburg, Germany and was renamed ALSTERDAM. The ship sailed under this name until 1912 when she

The interior of the Island Carrier after her return to Island Tug and Barge.
The trees and bushes that had grown in her ballast had to be cleared out
before repairs could be made to damage from the fire.

Courtesy of Frank A Clapp

was sold to another German firm, F.A. Vinnen and Company of Bremen and was renamed ADOLPH VINNEN.

The ADOLPH VINNEN sailed under the ownership of the Vinnen Company until war was declared in 1914. She was loaded with coke in Hamburg and set sail on June 21 for the Mexican port of Santa Rosalia under the command of Captain Willy Muller. The crew had signed on for a voyage "to Santa Rosalia, further and back," but few of them would ever return to Germany. The war in Europe had started about the time that the ship was crossing the equator, but no one aboard would find out until three months later. On September 13 she met with another German sailing vessel and the crew were told of the declaration of war. Finally, on November 10, the ADOLPH VINNEN arrived at her destination in the Gulf of California after a journey of 142 days.

The ship's cargo of coke, destined for the copper smelters of Santa Rosalia, was unloaded and the cap-

tain waited for instructions on how he should proceed. He waited for a long time. The ADOLPH VINNEN and 12 other German Cape Horn windjammers were kept interred in Santa Rosalia for the duration of the war. They never returned to Germany. As the months and years passed, the crews and officers gradually left their ships, many finding work and settling in Mexico.

After the First World War, the ADOLPH VINNEN was awarded to Italy as part of war reparations forced on the Germans. However, the ship was never delivered to her new owners and was eventually purchased by Robert Dollar and Company of San Francisco on February 9, 1921 along with the other German ships from Santa Rosalia. The big barque was renamed MAE DOLLAR after the wife of A. Melville Dollar.

The MAE DOLLAR was operated under the ownership of the Robert Dollar Company until February 17, 1930 when she was sold to the Canadian Robert Dollar Company of Vancouver. Her registry was changed to the Canadian flag and she was renamed PACIFIC CARRIER the next day. The big steel barque's masts were removed and her spacious hull was opened up for use as a log, chip, and hog fuel barge. Coincidentally, the superintendent on the job of converting the vessel to a barge was Captain Daniel MacDonald, who had sailed on her as a young bosun many years before. The PACIFIC CARRIER was sold again to Pacific (Coyle) Navigation Company of Vancouver on April 30, 1934. They continued using her to supply the mills around coastal British Columbia.

The big steel barge received her sixth name on June 1, 1936 when she was sold to Island Tug and Barge Company of Victoria and was renamed IS-LAND CARRIER. Island Tug and Barge used the barge exclusively for transporting hog fuel and chips and the former windjammer was fitted with a conveyor belt system for handling these materials. She was kept busy right through the Second World War supplying mills around the coast of British Columbia and Washington.

The end of the ship's history nearly came late in 1944 when her load caught fire at Port Alberni. The fire was so intense that the ISLAND CARRIER had to be sunk in the Alberni Canal to extinguish it. The barge was refloated and towed to Sydney, where she remained while the management of Island Tug and Barge decided her fate. There was little damage to the ship's hull, but the conveyor system had been destroyed and the remaining decking and hull cross members had been twisted and deformed by the heat of the blaze.

On November 2, 1945 W.B. Scoular of the Powell River Company inspected the hulk to see if she was a candidate for use in the floating breakwater. Island Tug and Barge were reluctant to sell the barge, first trying to make a deal in which the Powell River Company would take her without charge on the condition that the towing company could have her returned if they found a use for her. After due consideration it was decided that the ISLAND CARRIER would be sold to the Powell River Company with the understanding that the towing company could buy her back with reasonable notice. A price of $9000 was agreed upon with a $500 charge for towing from Sidney. On December 15, 1945 the ISLAND CARRIER under tow of

the tug, SNOKOMISH arrived at Powell River to join the breakwater.

The hulk was ballasted with sand, gravel, and sludge from the bottom of the log pond, a material that was convenient because dredging was in progress at the time of her arrival. The ex-windjammer was anchored off the bow of the HURON where she remained for about eight years.

Island Tug and Barge decided to get the vessel back from the Powell River Company in 1954 and return her to work as a barge. The ISLAND CARRIER was exchanged for the hulk of the HMCS COATICOOK at no cost to the Powell River Company. Island Tug and Barge then sold the barge to Badwater Towing Company, Limited, a subsidiary of Crown Zellerbach Corporation, on April 27, 1954.

The old ship's strong hull was still in good condition and she had many more years of service ahead of her, but first she had to be put back into shape. In dry-dock at Victoria the work began. Damage from the fire was repaired and an accumulation of sea life was scraped from her bottom. The ballast that had been dumped into her hull had to be removed, but first trees — some as high as 15 feet tall — and underbrush that had grown in the rich soil from the

The Island Carrier, renamed Crown Zellerbach No. 1, was the only one of the Hulks to return to work on the sea.

Jack Cash photo

bottom of the log pond were cut down and disposed of. The vessel was overhauled. Five beams that supported the sides of her hull were replaced with three stronger beams, clearing space to allow her to carry logs up to 45 feet in length.

The reconditioned barge was sold to The Canadian Tugboat Company Ltd. on May 15, 1955 and on October 31, 1956 the ISLAND CARRIER was renamed CROWN ZELLERBACH #1. The barge worked under this name for the rest of her career.

On July 17, 1967, CROWN ZELLERBACH #1 was sold to Capital Iron & Metals Company of Victoria who resold her in 1969 to an U.S. buyer. The old ship was supposed to be towed to Alaska for use as a floating pier during construction of the Alaska pipeline, but this was never to take place. Finally, in 1971 the once proud sailing vessel was towed to Seattle where she was cut up for scrap, ending nearly 80 years of toil on the sea.

Fragments of the old barque are still in existence at several maritime museums along the West Coast. A section of her hull plating forms part of an exhibit at the San Francisco Maritime Museum; one of her anchors is on display in the park adjacent to the Vancouver Maritime Museum; and her rudder is at the Columbia River Maritime Museum at Astoria, Oregon. These pieces of the former merchant ship remain as relics of the bygone age of sail. ⚓

5

The Steel Ships

A modern fleet of ships does not so much make use of the sea as exploit a highway.

Joseph Conrad, The Mirror of the Sea

After the acquisition of the ISLAND CAR-RIER, the managers of the Powell River Company continued to actively seek more ship's hulks to use around the mill's log pond. No more wooden ships would be brought to Powell River for the breakwater — the lessons of the BLATCHFORD and the MALAHAT had been learned. Steel-hulled ships only were to be considered for use.

With the end of the Second World War, vast numbers of new tankers and cargo ships were released from their war-time commitments. This allowed many older ships that had been kept in service past their normal life span to be decommissioned and released to the scrap-yards. Many warship hulls also became available when they were no longer needed in the smaller peace-time navy. The steel hulks that were purchased by the company over the next 15 years were of four very different types of ships. An ancient tanker, a coastal patrol vessel, a Royal Canadian Navy frigate, and a Union Steamship all found their way into the break-water fleet.

In 1918, with the war over, the WINNIPEG was sold again, this time to Standard Oil of New Jersey. She was renamed CADDO and was registered in New York. The CADDO sailed for Standard Oil until 1929 when her ownership was transferred to Imperial Oil Limited, a Canadian subsidiary of Standard Oil.

Imperial Oil renamed the tanker ALBERTOLITE, the second of the company's ships to bear that name.

The Imperial Oil tanker Albertolite in Vancouver Harbour.

Vancouver Maritime Museum

SS Albertolite

In the great shipbuilding city of Newcastle upon Tyne, England, Armstrong and Whitworth & Company launched the 415 foot long oil tanker, ADORNA in 1912. Built for Deutsch-Amerika PetroleumGes, and registered in Hamburg, the ship was of 6330 gross tons, had a beam of 55 feet, and was 31 feet in depth. The tanker was steam powered and was fitted with four-cylinder, triple expansion engines of 597 net horsepower.

The ADORNA sailed under the German flag until 1914 when she was renamed WINNIPEG and registered in Ottawa under the British flag. The ship was owned by the International Petroleum Company Ltd. The tanker spent the years of the First World War braving the killing grounds of the North Atlantic and managed to survive the war relatively unscathed, despite many crossings.

They moved the ship to the Pacific where she operated right through to the end of the Second World War, bringing crude oil from South American and Californian ports to her homeport at Ioco, British Columbia. Captain A.A. Mosher commanded the ship through much of her career.

The normal life span of an oil tanker was about 25 years and the ALBERTOLITE was already past this age when World War II started in 1939. Even so, the slaughter of allied merchant ships by the U-boats in the Atlantic made vessels of this type valuable at any age, and many old tankers were patched up as well as possible and sailed throughout the war. Such was the case with the ALBERTOLITE, which was by then the oldest ship in Imperial Oil's fleet of ten ocean-going tankers.

After the Japanese attack on Pearl Harbor in 1941, the West Pacific became a very hazardous place for allied shipping. Through December 1941, Japanese submarines attacked many merchant vessels along the American West Coast, sinking several. They returned in June 1942, and again terrorised ships along the West Coast, from Alaska to California. By this time the majority of merchant vessels had been lightly armed with guns for defence from submarines. Naval volunteers known as DEMS (Defensively Equipped Merchant Ship) gunners manned these deck guns, assisted by the merchant ship's crew members. Unlike the convoys operating in the Atlantic, the Pacific-based ships sailed alone and, armed or not, sailing the West Coast of North America was very dangerous.

The ALBERTOLITE's only encounter with a Japanese submarine came in October 1942. The tanker had taken on a load of crude oil at Avila, California when Captain Mosher ordered the crew back to the ship. Enemy submarines had been reported off the coast of Oregon. The Japanese submarine I-25 had sunk two American tankers and the captain wanted to get back to Vancouver as soon as possible. One night during the passage back to BC, the ringing of the ship's alarm bells and the sound of her engines slowing down roused the crew. The ship was hidden in shadow from the clouds as the DEMS gunner and the crew manned the gun on the ALBERTOLITE's stern. Out on a moonlit patch of water, the low outline of a submarine could be seen. The tanker's crew could even hear the voices of the submarine's crew as they lay on the surface. The gunner waited for the order to open fire on the enemy vessel, but Captain Mosher opted to hold off in hopes that they could avoid a battle that the old tanker would certainly lose.

The I-25 was a dangerous adversary for a merchant vessel, being armed not only with deck guns and torpedoes, but also with a small floatplane that was stored in a watertight hangar. The plane was launched using a catapult. The I-25's plane had actually been used to drop incendiary bombs on the coastal forests of Oregon during September 1942, setting several small forest fires and marking the first time that the American mainland had ever been bombed.

After about half an hour the submarine moved off and the ALBERTOLITE continued home without further incident. It is not known if the submarine did not see the tanker lying in the shadows or whether the sub's captain decided not to attack for some undetermined reason.

As the war in the Pacific progressed, the threat from submarines on the West Coast of North America lessened. The ALBERTOLITE survived the war without any more contact with the enemy. The end of the Second World War brought a glut of new, more efficient

ships that had been released from the wartime merchant navy. Imperial Oil sold the ageing tanker, already well past her design life span, to Capital Iron and Metals Company of Victoria in 1946. Here she was stripped and, in the fall of 1946, purchased by the Powell River Company at scrap rate — 1200 tons

The hulk of Albertolite in the Powell River breakwater.

NorskeCanada Millennium Project

at $6 a ton — for a total of $7200. In December 1946 the hulk of ALBERTOLITE arrived to take her place in the Powell River breakwater. She was moored next in line to the ISLAND CARRIER, enlarging the breakwater to four ships. The ALBERTOLITE remained in this place until 1960. By this time her hull had begun to rust through and she was in danger of sinking so the old tanker, survivor of two World Wars, was towed to Seattle and was cut up for scrap by Commercial Metals, Ltd.

CGS Malaspina

The next arrival at Powell River was the smallest of all the ships that were used as breakwater hulks at the mill's log pond. The Dublin Dockyard Company of Dublin, Ireland, had built the Fisheries Protection Cruiser MALASPINA in 1913. The Department of Marine and Fisheries, precursor to many of today's Canadian Government organisations, like Fisheries and Oceans Canada, the Canadian Coast Guard and even the Royal Canadian Navy, had ordered the MALASPINA and her sister ship, GALIANO, for patrol duties around the British Columbia coast. The two vessels had been assigned to protect the fishing industry from foreign and resident poachers and to control the flow of illicit goods being smuggled from the U.S.

The MALASPINA was 162 feet long, had a 27-foot

beam, and a draft of 13 feet, and was of 392 gross tons. A triple expansion engine of 1350 indicated horsepower powered her single screw, and could push her to a speed of 14.5 knots. The ship's bunkers could hold up to 200 tons of coal to keep her boilers fired during extended cruises. To back up her authority as an arm of Canadian law, the MALASPINA mounted a single, quick firing Hotchkiss 6-pounder

The Canadian Government Ship Malaspina.

NorskeCanada Millennium Project

gun on her forward deck. A complement of 40 officers and crew manned the ship when on patrol.

The MALASPINA arrived in BC in early 1914 and immediately went into service patrolling the inlets and islands of the coast. This could be a perilous duty in the days before accurate charts, radar, and Global Positioning Satellites. The shoreline and hidden rocks, often fog-shrouded, claimed many boats and ships in the early years of coastal navigation. Captain Newcombe, MALASPINA's master for many years, was asked once how he knew where he was after being enveloped in dense fog for days at a time. "Well, I put my hand out and pluck some leaves off a tree and I can tell where I am by the kind of leaves I get," he replied.

One of the duties assigned to the cruiser was the prevention of liquor smuggling into British Columbia from the U.S. during prohibition in Canada. Several American rumrunners were arrested by the ship, and escorted into port where their cargo was seized. While dockyard workers unloaded the contraband,

many cases would mysteriously disappear, slipped over the side to be reclaimed at low tide. It is rumoured that the crew of the MALASPINA was not above the occasional libation of confiscated liquor as well.

When Canada declared war in August 1914, the Navy commandeered the MALASPINA for war service. The Fisheries ship worked as a minesweeper and minelayer on the West Coast, and guarded wireless stations along the coast. She also served as a tender to the fleet, including the Japanese heavy cruiser IZUMO, which had been stationed in Barkley Sound to guard the Bamfield Cable station from possible German attack. The Japanese, our allies in the First World War, assigned their fleet to protect the Canadian West Coast.

It was during this period of her career that the MALASPINA had one of her first encounters with Powell River. At that time, the town was completely isolated from the rest of the province by geography and was dependent on the arrival of steamships a few times weekly for the transportation of supplies and people. The Powell River Company had run a telegraph wire to Vancouver to allow communication with its head office when needed. But they found that the line, which ran through the forests between the town and the city, was broken almost every time a storm blew up. To allow an uninterrupted link between the mill and head office, the company had, during the first few years of its operation, invested in a private radio station that they could use while waiting for repairs to the telegraph line.

During the First World War, all private use of radio equipment was banned, forcing the company to depend solely on the telegraph. The story goes that after a particularly long period with no contact from Vancouver (the cable being out of commission yet again), a company official authorised the use of the radio station to send a message. Within a few hours the MALASPINA steamed into sight, dropping anchor just outside of the log pond. A boat was launched and filled with an armed party of about a dozen sailors. It was dispatched to the dock where the landing detail formed up and marched up the hill to the mill office, their officer in the lead.

Arriving at the office, the ship's officer declared that

he had been sent to seize the radio and ordered the mill's assistant manager to hand it over immediately. The assistant manager, eyeing the armed group of sailors, agreed to turn the set over right after lunch. The officer at that point directed the manager's attention to the ship anchored in the harbour which had its gun trained on the radio's antenna atop the acid tower. A simple wave of his handkerchief out the office window, he said, would signal the ship to open fire. Not surprisingly, a crew worked through their lunch-time to remove the radio set, and the ship's party marched back down the hill with the offending piece of equipment. They returned to their ship and sailed away.

Captain Newcombe had demonstrated that he was not afraid to use the 6-pounder on the deck of the MALASPINA. A foreign fishing vessel that had been caught working inside Canadian territorial waters dropped her gear and tried to run, ignoring orders to stop and several warning shots fired over her bows. Finally, Captain Newcombe ordered the gunner to disable the boat's engine. A shot fired through the fishing boat's side stopped her, but resulted in the death of one of the boat's crewmembers.

The MALASPINA carried on with her patrol duties in the period between the two World Wars, serving the Department of Transport. Canada's entry into World War II saw the MALASPINA commissioned into the Royal Canadian Navy once again. She was assigned to patrol and inspection duty, this time with the added threat of Japanese submarines to concern her. Later in the war, the ageing ship was taken over by HMCS Royal Roads as a training vessel.

On March 31, 1945 the MALASPINA was paid off and the following year she was sold for scrap. Stripped of her equipment and superstructure, the hulk of the former Fisheries cruiser was purchased by the Powell River Company at scrap rate — 160 tons at $6 a ton — for a total of $960. She arrived at Powell River in December 1946 and was ballasted with crushed limestone. It was originally thought that the MALASPINA would be used to protect the gap between the rock breakwater and the hulk of the CHARLESTON, where there had been plans to place the MALAHAT. However, the boomsticks that had been placed across the gap were doing an adequate job of breaking the waves there. The MALASPINA ended up taking station on the opposite end of the

The hulk of the Malaspina, dwarfed by the new concrete ships, protects the north end of the log pond in 1948.

NorskeCanada Millennium Project

breakwater, near the log hauls for the sawmill. As Oren Olson said, "We used the MALASPINA right at the sawmill to keep the water quiet." The small hulk remained there, keeping the water calm and serving as a mooring point for hog fuel and chip barges until June 29,1949, when she sank at her moorings next to the dock. She remained on bottom for nearly two years.

On May 21, 1951 the hulk of the MALASPINA was raised from the bottom of the log pond. Slings, placed around the hull by divers, were attached to a huge spruce log that had been laid across two barges. At low tide the slack on the slings was taken up and the rising tide was supposed to lift the hulk off the bottom. But the old Fisheries boat had settled into the mud and didn't budge. The big spruce log was driven down into the barges by the tide, causing considerable damage. Finally, using cranes, barges and pumps, the MALASPINA was coaxed off the bottom and refloated.

Whether she was sent to the shipbreakers for scrapping or towed offshore and scuttled, the fate of the hulk of the MALASPINA is unknown at this time. The Fisheries Protection Cruiser figured greatly in the maritime history of British Columbia, serving through two World Wars and the years between, protecting our resources and sovereignty. All that remains of her are photographs, a model at the Vancouver Maritime Museum, and her rich legacy of service, carried on today by the Canadian Coast Guard.

The Malaspina was raised in May 1951. Afloat after two years on the bottom, the fate of her hulk is unknown.

NorskeCanada Millennium Project

HMCS Coaticook (K 410)

With the hulk of the MALASPINA gone, the log pond near the log hauls had less protection. The small hulk had worked well in that spot, providing much-needed moorage space for hog fuel and chip scows. Management at the mill wanted to find another ship to use in that position and the hulk that filled the spot was that of the Canadian River Class Frigate, HMCS COATICOOK. The COATICOOK was one of 11 River Class Frigates that were paid off and scrapped after the war, and then sent to various booming grounds and log ponds in British Columbia for use as breakwater hulks.

Davie Shipbuilding and Repairing Company Ltd. built the COATICOOK at Lauzon, Quebec, as part of the 1943 — 44 expansion program of the Royal Canadian Navy. She was launched on November 26, 1943 and was commissioned on July 25, 1944 at Quebec City. She was given the wartime pendant number K 410.

At Canada's entry into World War II on September 10, 1939, the country's navy was ill equipped to deal

The River Class Frigate HMCS Coaticook in 1945.

Edward W Dinsmore photo, National Archives of Canada

with the realities of modern warfare of the time. The only Canadian vessels suitable for wartime escort duty were six destroyers. This small navy grew throughout the course of the war into the third largest naval force in the world as a result of rapidly expanding programs of domestic shipbuilding.

The first type of vessel built in Canada for escort duty was the Flower Class Corvette. These small ships had been designed for coastal use but, because they could be built quickly and in large numbers, were used as ocean escorts until better-suited ships could be designed and built for that purpose. In that task the Corvettes and their crews performed heroically, escorting convoys in the North Atlantic and battling the German U-boats.

A British design, originally called the Twin Screw Corvette, was eventually settled on as a replacement for the Corvette. The Twin Screw Corvette was later renamed the River Class Frigate. A total of 60 of these larger, better-armed escorts were built for the Royal Canadian Navy.

The River Class Frigates were 301 feet, 6 inches long, had a beam of 36 feet, 7 inches, and a draft of 12 feet, 9 inches. They displaced 2218 tons at full load. A crew of eight officers and 133 men lived aboard the ships when at sea. These vessels must have seemed very roomy to the men who were accustomed

The hulk of the Coaticook took the place of the Malaspina in the breakwater.

Powell River Historical Museum

to sailing on the much smaller Corvettes.

For armament, the Frigates carried one twin 4-inch gun, one 12-pounder, and four twin 20-mm guns, arranged in pairs. As anti-submarine weapons, four depth charge throwers were mounted, as were a pair of depth charge traps. The ships carried 150 to 200 depth charges. The Frigates were also equipped with the latest in anti-submarine defence, the Hedgehog.

hulk was towed to Powell River where she took the MALASPINA's position in the breakwater. She remained there for seven years.

In 1961, her hull rusting through, the hulk of the COATICOOK was sold back to Capitol Iron and Metals for scrapping. While she was being towed to her destruction, a storm blew up and the Frigate's hull began to take on water. When she arrived at Victoria,

A huge explosion blows the bottom out of the Coaticook off Race Rocks, near Victoria.
She sinks quickly, never to be seen again.

Courtesy of Ronald Greene

This forward-firing device launched a cluster of explosive charges that would detonate on contact with a U-boat, unlike depth charges, which were pre-set to explode at a certain depth. Firing the explosives ahead of the ship meant that the U-boat could be attacked while still in the sight of the ship's SONAR, or ASDIC, as it was known then. When Hedgehog charges exploded a hit was a certainty, and a kill could be confirmed by the image shown on the ASDIC. Depth charges, on the other hand, would explode at the depth to which they were set and confirmation of a kill was hard to establish.

The COATICOOK was assigned to Escort Group 27, Halifax in September 1944. From then, and until the end of the war in Europe, she performed patrol and convoy escort duties from that port. In June 1945, the Frigate was ordered to the West Coast where she was paid off and placed in reserve at Esquimalt on November 29, 1945. In 1948 the COATICOOK was sold for scrap to Capitol Iron and Metals Company of Victoria.

Island Tug and Barge purchased the COATICOOK to exchange for the ISLAND CARRIER when they wanted to return the former windjammer to service as a barge. In late1953, the COATICOOK's stripped

an inspection revealed that her hull had split open. Rather than risk having the hulk sink at the dock the decision was made to tow the hulk away from Victoria and scuttle her in deep water.

Just off Race Rocks four cases of Forcite explosive were put into the COATICOOK's hull. That was much more dynamite than was needed to sink her, but nobody wanted to take any chances. When the explosives were set off, the Frigate's bottom was blown out, and onlookers from the tug that had towed her there were bombarded with mud and debris. A large piece of the COATICOOK flew right over the tug. The former sub-chaser sank quickly by the stern and was never seen again. Photographs of the COATICOOK's destruction were published in newspapers across the country, a spectacular end for a once-proud ship.

SS Cardena

The last steel hulk purchased for use in the mill's breakwater was a familiar ship to the people of Powell River. The steamship CARDENA at one time had been the flagship of the Union Steamship Company's fleet. She had served the cities, towns, villages and camps of the British Columbia coast for more than three decades and was considered by many to be the most beautiful vessel of her day.

Built by Napier and Miller of Old Kilpatrick, Scotland on the Clyde River, the CARDENA was launched in 1923. She was 226 feet, 8 inches in length, had a beam of 37 feet, 1 inch, and was 18 feet, 4 inches deep. She was of 1559 gross tons. The ship was equipped with a pair of triple expansion engines of 2000 indicated horsepower that could drive her to a top speed of 14 knots. The CARDENA was licensed to carry 150 passengers and could carry 350 tons of cargo. She was also equipped with a new innovation for the coast, a refrigerated hold that was capable of keeping 30 tons of boxed fish frozen.

The CARDENA sailed from her builders in Scotland on May 3, 1923 and arrived in Vancouver on June 11. Nine days later she began her career, replacing the old CHELOHSIN on the northern route, servicing the coast between Prince Rupert and Vancouver. She

aground and was hung up on the notorious Ripple Rock. She was in very serious danger, close to the cliffs of the Narrows in a strong tide, and she was carrying a full load of passengers. The CARDENA's captain, in an outstanding display of seamanship, brought the ship in close to the PRINCE RUPERT and had a line heaved to the crippled ship. Once the line was fastened to the CNR ship's stern, the CARDENA came alongside and tied to the ship's port side, pulled her off the rock and towed her to Deep Cove, a mile away. There the passengers and mail were transferred to the CARDENA, and to the Canadian Pacific Railway's steamship, PRINCESS BEATRICE, which happened to be sailing by. The gallant performance by the CARDENA and her crew marked the beginning of a string of bad luck that plagued the vessel for the remainder of her career. She herself went aground and had to be rescued several times.

In 1929 the ship ran aground on a sand bar in the Skeena River slough, and it took two days to free her.

The Union Steamship Cardena.

Vancouver Maritime Museum

carried people and the necessities of life to widespread logging camps, canneries and settlements, small and large.

The CARDENA came to national attention on August 22, 1927 because of an incident involving the Canadian National Railway's steamship, PRINCE RUPERT, in Seymour Narrows. The CNR ship had run

Little damage was done, but on her next excursion she ran aground on Village Island in the Skeena River. In the early 1930s, when approaching the wharf at Namu, the chain on the CARDENA's engine telegraph broke. Unable to signal the engine room to stop, the steamship powered right into the BC Packers freighter, P.W., cutting the freighter in two at the dock.

Luckily the P.W.'s crew had been warned by whistle blasts from the Union Steamship, and they managed to escape before the collision.

In 1942, under wartime blackout conditions, the CARDENA was rammed by the tug, LA POINTE in Goletas Channel. The steamship was seriously damaged but miraculously there was no loss of life. The passengers thought at first that a Japanese submarine had torpedoed them as such a vessel had recently shelled the lighthouse at Estevan Point. The crew reacted very professionally, and the passengers were loaded into the lifeboats to be picked up eventually by an American yacht that took them to Port Hardy.

In 1948 the CARDENA went aground again, this time on the rocks at False Bay. Damage in this grounding was quite serious, punching holes in two of her holds and one of her fuel tanks. On November 11, 1950 the steamship grounded again and got stuck in the sand of Savary Island while approaching the dock. She

floated free on the rising tide, but later the same day went up on the rocks at Surge Narrows, pushed ashore by a strong tide. For the second time that day she floated free on the rising tide.

In 1952 on a trip from Powell River, the CARDENA went aground on the mud flats near the mouth of the Capilano River while trying to avoid another vessel. She was pulled free with little damage. This was not the case in 1953 when she hit a rock in Patrick Passage en route to Sullivan Bay. The ship was badly holed, but managed to return to Vancouver under her own power.

Later in 1953, while in a dense fog, the CARDENA had a very serious head-on collision with the CPR steamship PRINCESS ELIZABETH under the Lion's Gate Bridge. Damage to both vessels was severe, but restricted to areas above the ships' waterlines. A 20-foot hole had been ripped in the CARDENA's bow, and her anchor was embedded in the CPR ship's bow. The two steamships had to be cut apart with torches

Passengers and crew crowd the decks of the CNR steamship Prince Rupert (L) at Deep Cove after her rescue from Ripple Rock by the Cardena (R).

Vancouver Maritime Museum

before they could head to the dock for repairs.

Late 1956 brought another grounding for the steamship when she went up on the rocks near Port Hardy, this time with minimal damage. This was the last of the ship's misadventures, and the last year of her service passed with no further mishaps.

While it may seem that the Union Steamship was somewhat accident-prone, the service that was provided by her, and others of her type, was invaluable. The steamships of British Columbia provided a lifeline for the people who lived and worked all along the coast, carrying all types of freight and supplies. Many of the families that settled in the coastal communities of BC saw their new homes for the first time

Throughout her career, the Cardena went aground many times, often being seriously damaged.

Vancouver Maritime Museum

from the deck of one of the Union or Canadian Pacific steamships. Loggers, fresh from the bush, relied on the steamers to take them from their remote camps back to the "big smoke," where they could blow off a little steam of their own.

During World War II the CARDENA, along with her sister steamships, was painted battleship grey and put to work supplying military bases and posts along the coast as far north as Alaska. This was in addition to handling her civilian duties. The ship worked without stop all through this period, through all kinds of weather, and under blackout at night.

The post-war years saw the gradual decline of the Union Steamship Company's fortunes.

The Kelsey Bay ship breakwater is the final resting-place of two former Powell River hulks. At the top of this photo is the large, partially submerged hull of the Charleston. The Cardena is the smaller ship on the inside of the upper breakwater.

Courtesy of Westmar Consultants Inc.

As many of the coastal communities became accessible by roads, ferries, and aircraft, passenger traffic fell off and made the steamships less profitable. Appeals for government subsidies to keep the company going were not forthcoming and by 1958 the CARDENA had been laid up. She lay rusting at her berth until late 1959 when she was put up for sale.

In February 1961 the Capital Iron and Metals Company of Victoria purchased the CARDENA. She was stripped down to her hull and purchased by MacMillan, Bloedel, and Powell River Limited, the company that succeeded the Powell River Company as owners of the mill, for a price of $12,500. The former Union Steamship was towed to Powell River in October to take the COATICOOK's place in the breakwater, near the log hauls.

By this time the breakwater at the mill had become the realm of the big concrete hulks. The CARDENA was the only steel hulk in the breakwater until about 1966. Around that time she was removed from the log pond and was towed to Kelsey Bay. There she joined the hulk of the CHARLESTON as part of the grounded ship breakwater at MacMillan Bloedel's booming ground. Her rusting hull can still be seen there today. ⚓

A 1948 aerial view of the log pond and breakwater looking south. The old government wharf extends into the centre of the log pond. The breakwater ships are, from upper left: the Charleston, Huron, Island Carrier, Albertolite, then the newly arrived concrete ships John Smeaton, L.J. Vicat, Armand Considere, and Henri Le Chatelier, and finally, the little Malaspina at the north end with a hog fuel barge tied to her.

NorskeCanada Millennium Project

6

American Concrete Shipbuilding

When a new idea or invention is first put into service, it is naturally received with a certain amount of antagonism. The concrete ship is no exception to this rule.

N.K. Fougner, 1922

By the end of 1948 the mill's breakwater began to be dominated by ships built of reinforced concrete. These enigmatic vessels gradually replaced the steel hulks. Their great weight in relation to their size, the chief factor that made them inefficient in operation compared to steel ships, made them ideal as floating breakwaters. The concrete hulks have outlasted any of their steel or wooden sisters, affirming of some of the claims made by their proponents during the development of their class.

The origin of concrete ships can be traced back to 19th Century France. Joseph Louis Lambot, in what is believed to be the first use of reinforced concrete, built two small rowboats in 1848 and 1849. These boats, which were built using wire mesh as a reinforcing material with a cement and sand mortar trowelled on to form the hull, were displayed at the Paris World Exposition in 1855 and survive to the present day in a museum at Brignoles, Provence, France. Lambot's boats sparked interest in the construction of floating structures using concrete. Barges, pontoons, lighters, and small motor and sailing boats were built in many nations around the world in the years between the 1850s and the First World War.

The first sea-going ship that was built of concrete was launched in 1917. Nicolay Knudtzon Fougner, a Norwegian civil engineer, built the 84-foot long motor ship, NAMSENFJORD. This vessel proved to be entirely seaworthy and earned recognition for concrete ships from Lloyd's Register of Shipping. Having proven the viability of the type, Fougner built several other successful concrete ships for use as small coastal freighters.

The First World War

The most significant force towards the development of ocean-going concrete ships came with the United States' entry into World War I. As mentioned in Chapter 3, the United States Shipping Board was formed in 1916 to promote the construction of ships and the expansion of the U.S. Merchant Marine. After the United States declared war in 1917, the Emergency Fleet Corporation was formed and given sweeping powers over shipyards and ship construction.

The idea of building ships out of concrete had been presented to the USSB, but none of the board's directors had been in favour of pursuing the matter because of the experimental nature of these craft. The directors of the USSB decided to concentrate their efforts toward the construction of steel and wood vessels. This, despite the fact that concrete ship construction used far less steel than would be needed for steel vessels and the steel that was used was in the form of reinforcing bar, which was of lower grade and relatively plentiful. The U.S. steel industry was not yet up to full wartime production and plate steel, which was needed for conventional ship construction, was in very short supply. Finally in December 1917, the Department of Concrete Ship Construction was formed to re-examine the possibility of building ocean-going steamships from concrete.

There was fervent lobbying going on to promote concrete ship construction and several prominent people and organisations endorsed the concept. In January 1918, a building contractor named Roy Robinson testified before the U.S. Congress Commerce Committee and extolled the advantages of ships built of concrete. Robinson claimed that concrete ships could be built faster than steel ships with less expense and utilising a less-skilled workforce. He also made the claim that a concrete ship that was hit by a torpedo would not sink, because the properties of concrete would localise the damage and any holes could be quickly patched up with a bit of cement. This impressive report was met with enthusiasm by many of the people who heard it. The general impression was that concrete shipbuilding was as simple as pouring concrete into some forms and popping out a ship a few days later.

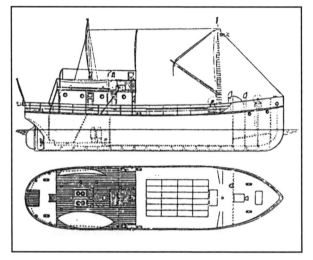

The Namsenfjord was the first self-propelled reinforced concrete ship.

Source unknown

N.K. Fougner's brother, Hermann, a resident of New York, travelled to Washington with plans for concrete ships in hand. With the USSB he saw the opportunity for a much larger market for his brother's work than was available in Norway. He presented the success of the NAMSENFJORD to the USSB as evidence of the role that concrete ships could play in the American merchant fleet.

The Portland Cement Company was also an advocate of the concrete ship concept. They circulated pamphlets that advertised the many advantages of concrete ships. They claimed that they were " fireproof, rat proof, would neither rot nor rust, were not susceptible to wood-boring worms, required practically no maintenance, could withstand very rough use, and could be built quickly and with less labour" than other types of ship. They also claimed that concrete construction was less expensive. The fact that housing starts were down and the company needed the extra business may have been a factor in their support.

Opponents of the concrete ship were many, and equally as vocal. Experts asserted that the greater hull weight of the vessels would make them slower, less efficient, and unable to carry as great a cargo as a steel or wood ship of similar size. They were unproven in operation and might be too rigid to withstand the stresses encountered in rough weather. It was also claimed that they would likely deteriorate with long exposure to seawater, and could disintegrate due to engine vibration. The experts questioned the idea that concrete ships could be built with less expense and more rapidly by unskilled labour, and they scoffed at the idea that the ships were immune

In 1917, work was begun on the Faith, the first American concrete steamship. Here, workmen assemble the reinforcing steel inside the outer hull forms.

U.S. National Archives & Records Administration

The 3500 D.W.T. concrete steamship, Cape Fear, was launched in July 1919. On October 29, 1920, she collided with another ship, "shattered like a teacup," and sank with a loss of 19 lives.

to attack by torpedoes. The uncertainty of whether U.S. industry was up to the task of supplying the boilers, engines, and other equipment that would be required for a fleet of concrete ships was another obstacle in the way of acceptance of this type of vessel.

Meanwhile, W. Leslie Comyn had established the San Francisco Shipbuilding Company in Redwood City, California. With little seasoned shipbuilding lumber and no steel mills on the West Coast, he had approached the USSB for funding to build concrete ships. He failed to convince the directors, but did receive exemption from the Emergency Fleet Corporation commandeering orders for the construction of this untried class of vessel.

Comyn managed to borrow enough money privately, and in September 1917 he started construction of the FAITH, the first American concrete steamship, and to that time, the largest concrete ship in the world. The FAITH was launched on March 14, 1918. She was 320 feet long, had a beam of 44 feet, 6 inches and was of 3427 gross tons. During her short career she made a considerable fortune for her owners, owing to her freedom from the Emergency Fleet Corporation's control. This allowed her to voyage to ports around the world during a time when there was a severe shortage of merchant ships. The success of the FAITH served as significant motivation toward

the construction of concrete ships in the United States.

The political pressure, the shortage of sheet steel, and the examples of Fougner's ships in Norway and the FAITH in California led the USSB to proceed with funding for the concrete shipbuilding program under the leadership of Rudolph Wig, a staunch supporter of the concrete ship. The original proposal was for the construction of 38 of these vessels, but most of them were never built. Like the wooden shipbuilding program, the end of the war resulted in the cancellation of most of the contracts, and only ships that were already under construction were completed. In total 12 ships were built as a result of the Emergency Fleet Corporation's concrete shipbuilding program, and none of them were launched before the end of the war.

War always causes acceleration of technological change, and the concrete shipbuilding program of the First World War resulted in many advances in the use of concrete. The Emergency Fleet Corporation enlisted the aid of the American Bureau of Standards and some of the best civil engineers of the day in their search for improvements to this unusual shipbuilding material.

Experiments in developing lightweight aggregate, using a vesicular slag made by burning clay and shale in kilns, lowered the weight of the concrete used to 107 pounds per cubic foot compared to 140 pounds per cubic foot for a traditional cement, sand, and gravel mix. Additives were formulated to make the new aggregate, known as "puffed brick", more workable and less brittle. To ensure that the batches of concrete used were of equal consistency, the "slump" test was developed. Progress was made in the design of reinforced concrete support beams, and new tools, such as pneumatic vibrators and hammers, were devised for working concrete into the forms. The growth of concrete technology during the World War I concrete shipbuilding program resulted in the development of procedures and processes that are still in use, and are considered to be engineering standards today.

The ships were designed by the USSB's naval architects. The first two were built in private yards for the Emergency Fleet Corporation and were considered experimental. The Fougner Concrete Shipbuilding Co., operated by the Fougner Brothers, built POLIAS — a ship of 2564 gross tons — at North Beach, Flushing Bay, New York, using a traditional concrete mix. The Liberty Shipbuilding Co. of Wilmington, North Carolina built ATLANTUS — a ship of 2391 gross tons — using the newly developed lightweight aggregate. The rest of the concrete steamships were built in yards owned by the Emergency Fleet Corporation and built specifically for the construction of concrete ships.

The next two ships were built to the Emergency Fleet Corporation's "3500 dead weight ton" design. The CAPE FEAR and the OLD NORTH STATE, later renamed SAPONA, were built by the Liberty Shipbuilding Company at Wilmington, North Carolina, and were very similar to the standard wooden "Ferris Ships" in lines and general arrangement. While these ships were under construction, the directors of the

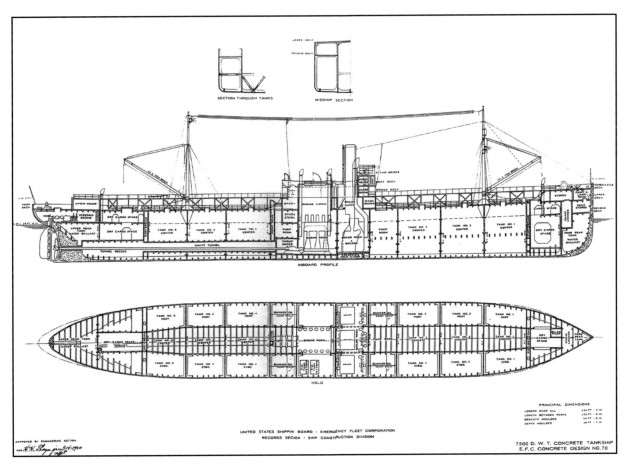

All eight 7500 DWT concrete steamships that were built for the Emergency Fleet Corporation were tankers. These are the general arrangement drawings for the Peralta.

Courtesy of Arthur R Herrick Jr.

USSB decided that the design was too small, and the remaining eight vessels built were of the corporation's "7500 dead weight ton" type.

All of the 7500 dead weight ton ships that were completed for the USSB were tankers. The design was 420 feet in length, had a beam of 54 feet, a depth of 36 feet and was of 6400 gross tons. The eight ships were built in four different shipyards. Fred T. Ley and Company built the SELMA and LATHAM in Mobile, Alabama. The San Francisco Shipbuilding Company, builders of the FAITH, built the PALO ALTO and PERALTA in Oakland, California. Pacific Marine and Construction Company built the CUYAMACA and SAN PASQUAL in San Diego, California. A. Bentley and Sons Company built the MOFFITT and DINSMORE in Jacksonville, Florida.

The hull of a concrete tanker took about 33 weeks to build and cost about $790,000. It took as much money again to equip and outfit the vessel, resulting in a total cost which was comparable to that of a steel ship of similar dead weight tonnage. While each of the shipyards varied the method of construction to suit their own circumstances, the general sequence for the construction of a concrete tanker was as follows:

1. The underpinning and blocking for supporting the floor forms was set in position on the ways.
2. Scaffolding with overhead trusses to hold the outside forms was set up.
3. The outside bottom and side forms were erected. This provided support for the reinforcing steel. The forms were built of cypress in the eastern yards and of Oregon pine in the west.
4. The steel inserts, such as the stern frame, hawse pipes, stem plate, and through hull fittings were attached in place on the inside of the outer forms.
5. The bottom and side shell steel reinforcing bars were put in place in the outside forms. The steel rods were round with a diameter that ranged between 1-3/8 inches and 3/8 of an inch.
6. The bottom and side frame steel and the keelson reinforcing steel was erected. Splice bars between the bulkheads and the shell were put in position.
7. The inside frame, keelson, and side shell forms were erected to a height of four or five feet.
8. Concrete was placed in the keelsons, the bottom, and sides of the frames and shell up to the four or five foot draft lines. The bottom concrete was five inches thick and the sides four inches.
9. After setting, the bottom inside forms were removed and the concrete was pointed up as

necessary. The top surface was thoroughly cleaned and roughened up to provide a good bond with the next pour.
10. Erection of the frame and bulkhead steel was continued up to the elevation of the second deck.
11. The inside frame, bulkhead, and shell forms were erected up to the second deck level, and inserts for piping and equipment were put in place.
12. Concrete was placed up to the underside of the second deck.
13. The inside forms were removed from the frames and bulkheads and the upper surfaces were roughened and cleaned.
14. Forms for the second deck beams and slab were placed, supported from below. Reinforcing steel and steel inserts for piping and equipment were put in position.
15. Concrete was placed for the second deck slab and beams.
16. The inside bulkhead and frame reinforcing steel was erected to the level of the top deck.
17. The inside shell, bulkhead, and frame forms were erected to the top deck level. Steel inserts were put in position as needed and the concrete was placed to the underside of the top deck. The upper surfaces of the concrete were roughened and cleaned.
18. The top deck beam and slab forms were put in position, inserts were positioned and reinforcing steel was put in place. Concrete was then placed for the top deck.
19. The reinforcing steel for the hatch coamings, bulwarks, and deck erections and the forms for them, were erected and filled with concrete.
20. All forms were removed and the concrete was cleaned, pointed, and patched as necessary. Patching was often needed, as large sections of concrete were known to fall off as the forms were removed.
21. The outside surface of the concrete was painted. The inside was also painted if time permitted.
22. The ship was launched. The FAITH, ATLANTUS and POLIAS were launched in the conventional, stern first way. All of the other ships were launched sideways.

The conclusion of the First World War made the new ships redundant and inevitably slowed down the progress of their construction. The last of the vessels was delivered in April 1921. Two 7500 dead weight ton ships that were in the early stages of construction, one at Mobile and another at Oakland were

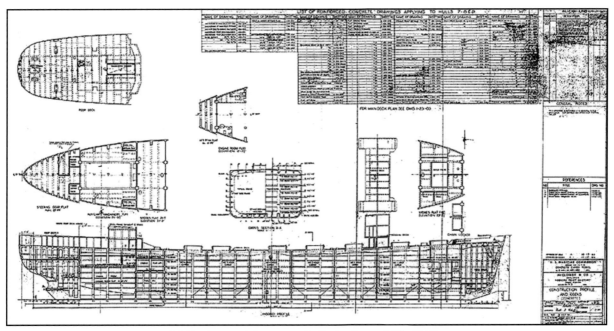

*McCloskey and Company built the Second World War
concrete steamships at Tampa, Florida.*

NorskeCanada

never completed. Both of these vessels were designed to carry general cargo.

In the period after the war three more concrete ships were launched by private enterprise. The MacDonald Engineering Works of Port Aransas, Texas built two unusual 298-foot long tankers for the France and Canada Oil Transport Company. The hulls of these vessels were basically a pair of 16-foot diameter concrete pipes, side by side, with a conventional hull built around them. Powered by Bolinder engines, they were only capable of a speed of three to five knots, and both ended up being abandoned. The last ship was a steam tanker of 3500 tons dead weight, launched as USQMC TANKER No. 1. This vessel, which was later named McKITTRICK, became one of the more notorious of the concrete ships. She ended her days as an offshore nightclub and casino.

The concrete shipbuilding program of the First World War was considered an unsuccessful experiment. The heavy ships could not compete with the numerous steel ships that became available after the end of hostilities, and none of them saw as much trade as the FAITH. In fact, some of the ships never traded at all. Most ended their days as breakwaters, piers and storage hulls.

That is not to say that from an engineering stand-

point they were a failure. The ships were found to be seaworthy and, counter to claims from their opponents, did not break up in heavy weather or disintegrate from engine vibration. The concrete hulls stood up well to exposure to seawater. When damaged, they proved to be relatively uncomplicated and inexpensive to repair. They were resistant to fire and explosion and the concrete hulls dampened vibration and had an easy motion in rough seas, making them pleasant to sail on.

The myth about the concrete ship being impervious to torpedoes was shattered tragically, however on October 29, 1920, when the CAPE FEAR collided with the steel steamship, CITY OF ATLANTA. According to a survivor, "She shattered like a teacup," and sank in three minutes in 125 fathoms of water, taking 19 men to the bottom.

Despite their general seaworthiness, the concrete ships were considered by many to be too unconventional, earning the nicknames "Floating Tombstones," "Floating Skyscrapers," and "Stone Ships." Many sailors refused to sail in them. An African American sailor probably expressed the sentiment best when he was signed up to go on board the OLD NORTH STATE on her way from the builders to the outfitters. His comment was, "I ain't gwine to sea on no grindstone!"

The Second World War

With the less than triumphant achievements of the First World War concrete ships, it is surprising that the Second World War saw the resurrection of concrete shipbuilding in the United States. The directors of the United States Maritime Commission (the successor organisation to the United States Shipping Board) presented the concrete ship as an alternative to steel ships during the plate steel shortage at the beginning of the war. This was not so much due to the virtues of the concrete ship, but more an attempt to avoid the type of wasteful fiasco that occurred with the wooden shipbuilding program of World War I. Admiral Emory S. Land, the chairman of the Maritime Commission, was so strongly opposed to concrete

ship construction that he threatened to resign his post. He withdrew his objection when he was faced with the scarcity of plate steel at the time.

The concrete used during construction of these vessels was heavier and richer than that used in the USSB's concrete shipbuilding program. It was composed of a lightweight aggregate, similar to that used during the First World War, mixed with between 15 and 50 per cent natural sand. One part cement to 2½ parts aggregate resulted in concrete that weighed about 115 pounds per cubic foot.

The construction sequence of the Second World War vessels was much the same as those of the First World War, the main difference being that the World War II ships were built in basins that were flooded to launch the hull. Forms were built of oil-treated plywood.

As in many wartime industries, women played a vital role in concrete shipbuilding. Here, female welders finish tacking the deck steel of a B7-D1 barge at Barrett and Hilp's Belair Shipyard.

U.S. National Archives and Records Administration

The side shell slabs were 6½ inches thick, deck slabs were 5½ inches, and bulkhead slabs were four inches thick.

During the Second World War, 104 vessels of five different designs were constructed. Only one of the designs was self-propelled; the other four being "dumb" or unpowered barges. The U.S. Maritime Commission designed the vessels and the builders made refinements to suit their requirements. Building contractors with experience in the construction of buildings, bridges, dams, and other structures using reinforced concrete formed the companies that built the concrete fleet of World War II.

Of the 104 concrete vessels built for the Maritime Commission, 24 were steam-powered cargo ships built by McCloskey and Company at the Hooker's Point Shipyard in Tampa, Florida. These ships were 366 feet in length overall, had a beam of 54 feet, and a depth of 35 feet. They displaced 10,950 tons and were designated as Maritime Commission type C1-S-D1. Approximately 3100 cubic yards of concrete and 1250 tons of reinforcing steel was used in the construction of each of these ships.

Barrett and Hilp built 20 unpowered bulk cargo barges in the Belair Shipyards at San Francisco. These vessels were also 366 feet in length overall, had a beam of 54 feet, and a depth of 35 feet. Designated as Maritime Commission type B7-D1, they displaced 10,970 tons. Each of the barges used 2600 cubic yards of concrete and 1100 tons of reinforcing steel.

Another type of unpowered barge was designated as Maritime Commission type B7-A1. These vessels had the same dimensions as the previous two, and were designed as tanker barges for the transport of oil products. MacEvoy Shipbuilding Corporation built seven of these barges at Savannah, Georgia. McCloskey and Company built another four at Houston, Texas. The B7-A1 barges were built using 2730 cubic yards of concrete and about 1520 tons of steel.

Concrete Ship Constructors of National City, California built the rest of the Second World War concrete vessels. The Maritime Commission B7-A2 type, another tanker barge, was the first type of concrete ship launched during World War II. These barges were 375 feet in length overall, had a beam of 56 feet, and were 38 feet in depth. They displaced 12,750 tons and used 3200 cubic yards of concrete and 1655 tons of steel bars. Twenty-two of them were built.

The last type of concrete ship, the B5-BJ type, was built in three different classifications. These were the smallest of the barges at 265 feet length overall, 48 feet in beam, and 17 feet, 7 inches deep. Each dis-placed 4000 tons and used 1125 cubic yards of concrete and 490 tons of reinforcing steel.

The construction of these vessels was an extension of the original concrete shipbuilding program and utilised a very simple flat slab design. Pre-cast concrete bulkheads were fitted into the hull after it had cured. This made a very strong, yet quickly built hull in comparison to the rest of the World War II concrete vessels, whose construction followed conventional ship design. One of these barges was actually built and launched in 6 ½ days.

The B5-BJ1 type barge was a double-decked, covered lighter and 22 were built. The B5-BJ2 was a modification of the B5-BJ1, and was equipped with 130,000 cubic feet of refrigerated space. Each of these barges could hold 1000 tons of meat, fruit, ice and ice cream, and they were used as food depots in the South Pacific. There were three of these built. The B5-BJ3 vessels, also modified from the B5-BJ1design, were outfitted as U.S. Army maintenance lighters. Only two of this type of barge were completed.

While the concrete steamships did see some service in the Merchant Navy, the majority of the Second World War concrete vessels were taken over by the U.S. Army and Navy for use in the Pacific. The tank barges were used as oil, gasoline and water storage and transport vessels. The others saw service as floating warehouses, training ships, and transports. Several of the ships were sunk in shallow water to provide protection for the landing of men and materials on the beachheads of the Second World War, both in Europe and the South Pacific. The end of the war resulted in most of them being withdrawn from service and eventually sold off for use as barges, piers, and storage hulls. Many of the vessels found their way into those unique sanctuaries of the concrete ship, breakwaters.

Since end of the war, concrete ship construction has been limited mostly to the building of ferro-cement yachts and workboats, a type of construction that saw great popularity with backyard builders. Concrete continues to be used for many types of floating structures, however, and the idea of concrete merchant ships is not dead. The thermal and physical properties of concrete have been found to make it a superior material for the storage of liquefied natural gas. Plans have been drawn for large ships and barges built of pre-stressed concrete for the transportation and storage of this cargo. Several have even been built, but whether we will ever witness another fleet of concrete merchant ships plying the world's oceans remains doubtful.

The concrete ships of the Powell River breakwater are likely the last of their types still afloat. Often mistakenly referred to as Liberty Ships, a term that has become generic when referring to any Second World War cargo vessel, they are in fact, examples of four different classes of ships and barges. Unusual, even at the time that they were built, they are unique examples of imaginative engineering and the quest for better and less expensive shipbuilding materials.

The concrete that was used in the construction of these ships continues to be of interest to experts in the construction field. Over the years many samples have been taken from all of the ships to analyse the condition of the concrete as it is exposed to time and the elements. Despite their dilapidated appearance, the ships have been found to be completely structurally sound. Engineers are perplexed by the longevity of the material used to build The Hulks and regard it as an example of the best lightweight concrete ever made. Experts in the field of concrete construction use standardised service life prediction techniques to estimate the life expectancy of concrete structures. When these techniques were applied to the concrete ships, they were only given an expected service life of 15 years, dating from the time of their construction. The concrete ships have once again proven the experts wrong, and settled the debate over the durability of concrete as a shipbuilding material once and for all. ⚓

Concrete being poured for the deck of a barge at Barrett and Hilp's Belair Shipyard. Great care was taken to ensure the quality of the concrete mix.

U.S. National Archives and Records Administration

7

The Concrete Steamships
of World War II

*Unquestionably the least popular ships built during the war
were the concrete ships, and the Army ended up with the
bulk of them...*

David Grover, US Army Ships and Watercraft of World War II

The managers of the Powell River Company continued their search for suitable ships to use in the breakwater after they acquired the ALBERTOLITE and the MALASPINA. By 1947 the U.S. Maritime Commission had started to sell off the surplus vessels of its Second World War "Victory Fleet," and company executives became aware of this vast armada of potential breakwater hulks. Nestled in among the scores of Liberty and Victory Ships, tankers and transports, was a small group of most unusual ships — the reinforced concrete steamships of World War II.

In the face of sheet steel shortages at the beginning of U.S. involvement in the Second World War, the U.S. Maritime Commission had awarded a $30 million contract to McCloskey and Company for the construction of 24 ships built of concrete. These cargo vessels were designed for the transportation of sugar from Cuba to ports around the Gulf of Mexico and the U.S. east and west coasts. Most of the freighters actually did work in that trade for a period of time, but as faster and more efficient steel ships became available, 22 of them were assigned to the U.S. Army for use as store ships, transports and training ships. Many of them operated in the Pacific war zone. To identify them as ships of the U.S. Army Transport Service, the designation U.S.A.T. preceded their names.

McCloskey and Company was a Philadelphia-based construction company with extensive experience in building structures made of concrete. The owner of the company, Matthew H. McCloskey Jr., a powerful Democratic politician and a personal friend of President Franklin D. Roosevelt, chose Tampa, Florida as the site for what became the Hooker's Point Shipyard. Hooker's Point is a sandy promontory that extends into Tampa Bay, and McCloskey chose it for three reasons. First was its proximity to the ship channel

An aerial view of the Hooker's Point Shipyard at Tampa, Florida. At the centre of the photograph, concrete ships can be seen in different stages of construction in the three long graving docks.

in Tampa Harbour. Second, the Florida Portland Cement Company, which was already completely equipped with the tools needed to mix and deliver

Workers lay out the reinforcing steel for one of the McCloskey and Company concrete steamships at the Hooker's Point Shipyard.

US National Archives and Records Administration

the necessary quantities of concrete, was its nearest neighbour. The last reason was the climate, which would allow year-round placing and working of the concrete.

In order to build the ships, a shipyard had to be built. In conventional shipyards, the ships are built on land and launched into the water. At Hooker's Point, however, three enormous concrete-lined basins, known as graving docks, were built. Each of them was 1200 feet long, 27 feet deep, and 82 feet wide. These basins, each large enough to allow the construction of three ships simultaneously, were connected to Tampa Bay at one end by huge doors. Once the ships under construction in a basin were ready to be launched, the doors were opened to allow water in. When the basin was full, the doors were opened wide and the ships could be removed for outfitting and sea trials.

In addition to the graving docks, buildings for offices, shops, and storage had to be erected. Access and service roads were also built. In order to accommodate the more than 1100 workers who were to be employed at the McCloskey yard, 600 housing units were built. This small community, known as Maritime Homes, was adjacent to the shipyard and included a grocery store, a theatre, barber and beauty shops, and other amenities.

A shipyard subculture arose in the Hooker's Point yard, and the residents of the housing project (the majority having been imported into Tampa to fill positions in the yard) considered themselves independent of and separate from the native Tampan population. Hooker's Point published their own bi-weekly newspaper, "The Hooker's Point Log," and sponsored their employees in a variety of sporting and cultural activities. As many women entered the work force, competitions were held to choose the best female welder. The winner was placed into competitions against other Eastern U.S. shipyards.

Once the infrastructure was in place, work began on the ships themselves. The U.S. Maritime Commission designed the concrete steamships and the McCloskey and Company engineers made any necessary modifications. As with the First World War concrete shipbuilding era, many improvements were made in the technology of shipbuilding with this unusual substance. The McCloskey engineers brought with them a great deal of experience in the construction of high-rise buildings, and applied their knowledge and techniques to the process of building the ships. Continuous pours of concrete were made possible using newly developed vacuum pumps and truck-mounted mixers. When a Hooker's Point engineer discovered that fuller's earth was a lighter-weight substitute for the sand that was usually used in concrete, McCloskey bought deposits and started a second industry for the mining of this material.

The Maritime Commission designated the ships as type C1-S-D1. These letters and numbers represented the characteristics of Maritime Commission vessels.

*The first three ships, Vitruvius, David O. Saylor, and Arthur Newell Talbot, are launched at
Hooker's Point on July 15, 1943.*

US National Archives and Records Administration

In the case of the concrete steamships, the "C1" indicated that the ship was a cargo vessel less than 400 feet in length. The "S" in the designation code indicated that the ship was powered by steam, was a single screw vessel, and had accommodations for less than 12 passengers (in addition to the crew). In the final group of figures, the "D" was a design letter that was associated with the ship's hull. The number "1" indicated that this was the original design. This number was changed with modifications to the structure or superstructure of a ship.

The ships were 366 feet, 4 inches in length overall, had a beam of 54 feet, and were 35 feet in depth. They had a dead weight of 5000 to 5200 tons and displaced 10,950 tons. The hulls were divided by ten transverse concrete bulkheads, creating seven dry cargo holds,

equipment space, and tanks. The poop and bridge decks were built of concrete; the deck housing was built of wood. Three rows of wooden fenders were anchored to the sides of each concrete hull and sheet steel protective plates were fitted to protect the bow and the area around the hawse pipes. The ships were painted a "low visibility grey" at the shipyard. Some were later painted olive green or blue-grey during their army service.

Each ship was equipped with two oil-fired watertube boilers, operated at 250 pounds per square inch. These boilers supplied steam to a single 1300 horsepower, triple expansion engine that spun a 14½-foot diameter, four bladed cast iron propeller to 80 RPM at full speed. Two steam turbine driven generators provided electrical power. All of the machinery

The SS Arthur Newell Talbot in service during WW II. The McCloskey and Company ships earned the nickname "Squatters" because of the way their aft-mounted equipment weighed them down at the stern.

Courtesy of Dr Mary Talbot Westergaard Barnes, State College PA

was located aft. The ships were capable of seven to nine knots, depending on their load, and had a cruising radius of about 28 days at cruising speed.

The freighters had a cargo capacity of about 233,000 cubic feet in their holds. On 15 of the ships, wood and steel decks were built in the holds to allow con-venient storage of general cargo. Fuel tanks held 3626 barrels of bunker oil. Saltwater ballast tanks held about 1240 tons of water. The ballast tanks were filled to prevent cracks from forming in the hull from stresses that were encountered when operating the ships with no cargo aboard.

A normal crew for one of the McCloskey ships was about 48 men, consisting of a mix of civilian Merchant Marine sailors, Army officers, and Naval Armed Guard gun crews. In the case of the ship U.S.A.T. HENRI LE CHATELIER, these were divided up thus:

Civilian: 38 men — 13 deck hands, 13 engineering, nine stewards, and three radio operators. Civillian sailors were of many nationalities. During U.S. Army service, the civilian crews were members of the U.S. Army Transportation Corps Water Division's "Civilian Branch."

Naval Armed Guard: six gunners.

Army: Master and three officers. Officers were regular Merchant Marine during operation with private shipping companies.

For safety, each ship was equipped with two galvanised steel motor-lifeboats, capable of holding 26 men each, two non-powered lifeboats that could carry 18 men each, four rafts that could hold 20 men each, and two eight-man life floats.

The ships were also equipped with a four person medical ward and a room for one "disturbed" patient. Crew quarters were located in the poop deckhouse above the boiler and engine spaces; the stack passed through the centre of the area. This resulted in warm accommodations during cold weather, but they were uncomfortably hot in warmer climates. The Chief Engineer of the

The USAT William Foster Cowham at an Australian port during WW II. The US Army used many of the concrete ships as storeships and transports in the South Pacific.

La Trobe Picture Collection, State Library of Victoria, Australia

SS JOHN SMEATON reported that his quarters reached a temperature of 120 degrees while steaming off the Canal Zone and the western coast of Mexico. Officer's quarters were located in the wooden bridge deckhouse.

As with most wartime merchant vessels, the concrete ships were armed for defence against submarines and aircraft. Typical armament consisted of two 30-mm guns mounted on the bridge deckhouse top and a six-pounder on the poop deck. Smoke floats were carried to provide a smoke screen in the event that the ship was attacked. For protection against magnetic mines, a degaussing system was installed. Controlled and monitored by the radio operators, these systems were fitted to merchant and naval ships alike. An arrangement of wires and cables that ran the length and breadth of the vessel were energised to cancel out the magnetic field produced by the metal in the ship.

All of the McCloskey and Company ships were named for men that had contributed to the development of concrete as a building material. The first group of three ships to be floated in their basin, VITRUVIUS, DAVID O. SAYLOR, and ARTHUR NEWELL TALBOT were gradually lifted from their blocking by the water let in from the basin doors on July 15, 1943. Unfortunately, the procedures that were needed to reduce uneven stresses on the hulls during flooding of the basin had not been properly worked out, and the VITRUVIUS and the DAVID O. SAYLOR both developed cracks in their side shells during the launching. This event probably led to these two vessels becoming the first of the World War II concrete steamships to be used as breakwaters. In April 1944, the VITRUVIUS and the DAVID O. SAYLOR crossed the Atlantic in a convoy. They were the only ships of their type to make this voyage. In June, a few days after the D-Day landings at Normandy, both ships were sunk, along with other old or damaged ships, to form a "gooseberry", an artificial harbour formed by sunken ships, at Utah Beach.

The rest of the ships at the Hooker's Point yard were launched without trouble. At peak production

rates, a group of three ships was launched every two months. The last of the concrete ships was launched on September 24, 1944. The total cost of building and outfitting the 24 ships was $48 million, almost $20 million over budget. Each vessel had an average price of about $2 million, a cost that was a bit higher than the $1.8 million required to build the significantly larger Liberty Ship.

By 1944, plate steel was plentiful and the time needed to build a concrete hulled ship (three to six weeks) made the type redundant, especially when Henry J. Kaiser was delivering a 450-foot long Victory Ship every ten days. The Hooker's Point yard went into production of steel ships for the duration of the war.

The men who sailed on the concrete steamships were of mixed opinion about their performance. Like their First World War predecessors, they were com-

The first four concrete ships shortly after their arrival at Powell River. John Smeaton is already anchored at the end of the breakwater with Armand Considere and L.J. Vicat, moored to her and Albertolite. Henri Le Chatelier is moored to the old government wharf.

NorskeCanada Millennium Project

fortable in stormy weather and vibration from the engine was minimal. A particular advantage of the concrete hull, as compared to steel, was the lack of condensation in the holds, a benefit that made the ships ideal for the transport of dry cargoes with little spoilage.

Minor repairs to the ships could be carried out while underway. Each vessel was fitted with bins for the storage of sand and aggregate and carried bags of cement in the bosun's stores. Richard R. Powers, a crewmember aboard the SS VITRUVIUS had this memory of his Trans-Atlantic crossing.

"We made the Atlantic crossing without any U-boat attacks — I guess they were too smart to waste torpedoes on us — but were rammed by a ship in our convoy. I will never forget the sight of the Bosun getting a sack of concrete to patch up the cracks." [Coincidentally, the ship that collided with the VITRUVIUS was the WILLIS A. SLATER, another McCloskey & Company concrete ship. The WILLIS A. SLATER returned to Bermuda for repairs and never made the trans-Atlantic crossing.]

At least three of the ships sailed through hurricanes with minimal damage. The SS JOSEPH ASPDIN encountered a hurricane off Cape Hatteras in 1944 and, although she was stripped of her lifeboats, apparently performed well in waves up to 80 feet in height.

The ships did seem to be prone to mechanical failures, however, and many of them lost rudders or propellers while at sea and had to be towed to safety. Problems were also encountered with cracks that developed in the concrete hulls and tanks. While leaks from these cracks were minor, the problem did cause a dispute between the U.S. Maritime Commission and McCloskey and Company over their builder's guarantee.

The ships were painfully slow and, like the concrete ships built during the First World War, were the subjects of suspicion and scorn. The McCloskey and Company ships earned the nickname, "Squatters," due to the ungainly stern down attitude caused by the weight of their aft mounted equipment.

The engineers that worked aboard the ships hated them almost unanimously. The insulating properties of the concrete hull made the boiler and engine rooms extremely hot and problems with the ships' electrical and mechanical systems were frequent. In the end it was their slow speed and great weight that made these ships unsuccessful, and the Second World War was the last time that concrete shipbuilding was undertaken to this extent.

James Moore was an oiler aboard the McCloskey and Company ship U.S.A.T. LEONARD CHASE WASON and gives this account of his impressions:

I hooked up with some of my buds at the Army Port of Embarkation, where we signed in at the "Vessel Manning Pool". This is a roster of Seamen kept on standby, to quickly fill any vacancies that may occur when an Army ship hits port. We were paid a small amount for subsistence and quarters, which kept us in beer and cigarettes, and a cheap place to live.

After two weeks of this easy living, several of us were told to report to the Concrete ship anchored in the river. I innocently asked, "Does it haul bulk concrete or bagged concrete?" The Port Director looked at me in disgust and said, "No, stupid that's what it is constructed from."

It was a sharp looking little ship, an engine aft freighter (like a tanker) about 350 feet long, and was very clean looking since concrete doesn't rust. Sadly, that's all the nice things I can think of to say about the SS Leonard Chase Wason.

At the time, we didn't realise how lucky we were that it was a short trip. Our destination was Norfolk, Virginia where the ship was to be laid up. Piece of cake, down the Mississippi and across the Gulf and ride the Gulf Stream up the East Coast and we would be there soon. Wrong! That chunk of rock drew 14 feet of water (empty) and was the most under-powered vessel since they built the MERRIMAC. At night it could have easily been mistaken for a lighthouse, 'cause it seemed like it never moved. When we were off the coast of North Carolina, a sea going tug, pulling almost a mile of tow [barges] passed us. Now that's embarrassing.

On my first visit to the engine room, I knew I was a dead duck. Here we are, sitting in port with one boiler banked and only the minimum of auxiliary equipment running, and the heat was unbearable. It's obvious that the thick concrete hull will not transfer the engine room heat to the surrounding seawater nearly as well as a three quarter inch steel hull will, so most of the BTUs generated down there were still there. Adding to the heat load was the simplistic design of some of the major equipment. The turbine generators were lagged with concrete instead of some heat insulating material, such as asbestos, therefore the heat from the steam turbine came right through this covering and would burn you if you touched it.

The ability of that thick concrete to trap and hold the heat carried over to the crew's compartments, so there was no let up in the heat. The officers living in the superstructure above the main deck had a different problem. Their part of the ship was constructed of plywood. All the seams in the housing had loosened up from the constant motion of the ship, therefore when it rained everything above the main deck was soaked. Officers soggy from the rain, or the crew soggy from the heat, it did not matter. Everyone was bitching their ears off.

At the end of the war, the concrete steamships were laid up in the various naval reserve yards on both coasts. The U.S. Maritime Commission removed the armament and ammunition from the vessels, and opened them up to bids from interested parties. The management of the Powell River Company identified these vessels as potential breakwater ships and purchased six of them from the Maritime Commission in 1947, issuing a requisition for $133,000. This price included the ships, anchors and chains, towing charges, and any consumable stores left aboard the vessels.

Of the six ships, the JOHN SMEATON, HENRI LE CHATELIER, L.J. VICAT, ARMAND CONSIDERE, THADDEUS MERRIMAN, and EMILE N. VIDAL, only four made the journey to Powell River right away. The THADDEUS MERRIMAN was kept laid up at Suisan Bay, California for a little more than one year before the company took possession of her. The Powell River Company sold the EMILE N. VIDAL to the Pennsylvania Salt Manufacturing Company (Pennsalt) shortly after they purchased her. Almost 20 years later, when Pennsalt Company had no further need of her, she found her way into the Powell River breakwater.

After receiving the first concrete ships, the Powell River Company realised that the concrete hulks were far superior to the steel hulks that had been used in the breakwater in the past. They continued to search for more, and in 1956 the P.M. ANDERSON also became the property of the company.

The arrival of the McCloskey and Company ships at Powell River caused a great deal of excitement among the local population. Unlike the stripped steel and wooden hulks that had been brought to the break-

Members of the Powell River Elks Club strip plywood from the cabin of one of the concrete ships, March 1948.

Powell River Historical Museum

water before, these were fully equipped merchant vessels, only a few years old. They still carried all the necessities of life at sea, from mechanical equipment and furniture, to bed linens in the cabins, and cutlery in the galley drawers. The management of the Powell River Company was very concerned about the possibility of theft from the ships. Their concern was reinforced when the Scott radio set was stolen from the L.J. VICAT somewhere between her berth at the Suisan Bay Naval Reserve yard and her arrival at Powell River. The FBI was called in to investigate, but whether the radio was ever recovered is unknown.

Company management had developed a procedure for dealing with the salvage of the goods aboard the ships. First, the company and its subsidiaries would identify and remove any materials that they could use from the vessels. The mill's instrument technicians removed instruments, such as pressure and temperature gauges, for use in the mill. One of the ship's compasses was removed and kept on hand as a spare for use on the company tug, TEESHOE. Among other assorted pieces of equipment that found their way into the mill, a public address system was salvaged and installed in the mill's steam plant. A pair of ice water coolers was taken for use at the company's head office in Vancouver. Lester W. Foley, the brother of the Powell River Company's president, was presented with the wheelhouse stand and engine room telegraph from one of the ships for use on his personal yacht in Florida.

The next step was to remove the rest of the salvageable goods from the ships and move them to the company gymnasium in the Townsite. Toilets, basins, beds and bedding, and other goods were priced and sold, first to company employees and then to the general public.

Local clubs and organisations were given permission to go aboard and strip materials from the ships that they could use. According to company documents, they were charged $1 for the goods that they removed from the vessels and were required to clean up after themselves. The Powell River Golf Club removed numerous wooden lockers from the ships for use in their clubhouse. Members of the Elks Club stripped plywood panelling from the cabins and used it to finish their new building. The Italian Club also removed plywood from the ships. The 11-ply panels were used to build a portable, 30-foot square dance floor that could be taken apart and transported to social events around the area.

The arrival of these "treasure ships" proved to be too tempting for some local residents and there was a rash of thefts. The antics have become the stuff of local legend, with stories of men stripping goods from the ships and dropping them down to boats, in some cases being operated by their wives. The mill's watchmen had trouble keeping up with this onslaught, and while they searched one ship for thieves, goods were being removed from the next one. Anything that wasn't bolted down (and much that was) was fair game. Some employees that were caught taking items from the vessels faced suspension from their jobs and there were reports of charges being laid. Powell River youth in particular found the ships to be an irresistible draw. Mill watchmen were also kept busy chasing the youngsters from these new and exciting arrivals to a small and isolated town.

Bob Monteith was a youngster, growing up in the Powell River Townsite when the ships arrived in the late 1940s. "The first place that we would head for was the lifeboats," he explained. "Each lifeboat had a survival kit and in the kit were tins, like the ones for canned ham. In the tins were blocks of the richest, most delicious chocolate that I ever tasted. I even took some home for my mother to bake with."

Later, when Bob worked in the log pond operating the log pond tugs, he salvaged wood from some of the ships that he used for flooring when he built his house. One interesting artefact in his collection is a milk bottle from a dairy in Tampa, Florida that was left aboard one of the vessels.

Finally, the company sold the remaining equipment aboard the ships for scrap. H.B. Wagner, I. Stein and M.L. Greene of Victoria, partners in Capital Iron and Metals, bought the remaining goods for $8500 on September 16, 1948. They agreed to have the work completed by February 28, 1949. They stripped almost everything else of value from the ships, leaving only a few pumps for emptying bilges and moving ballast. Dealing with the material aboard the first four ships was such a headache that Powell River Company management decided that any other ships brought to join the breakwater would be stripped before they arrived at Powell River.

SS John Smeaton

The steamship JOHN SMEATON was named after the Englishman who is considered the father of the civil engineering profession in Britain. Smeaton is famous for his work in building canals, bridges, and lighthouses, and was a leader in the development of steam power. He rediscovered hydraulic cement, a material that is able to harden underwater, and that had been lost since the fall of Rome. He used this substance as a jointing material when he rebuilt the Eddystone Lighthouse near Plymouth.

The SS JOHN SMEATON was launched on November 28, 1943 along with sister ships LEONARD CHASE WASON and JOSEPH ASPDIN. The ship was McCloskey and Company hull #8, and cost slightly more than $2 million to build. Her outfitting was completed and sea trials took place on April 11, 1944.

The JOHN SMEATON was registered on April 13, 1944, and was delivered to the War Shipping Administration. They placed her under contract with A.H.

The John Smeaton arrives at Powell River.

Powell River Historical Museum

Bull Steamship Company. The JOHN SMEATON worked in the sugar trade. Her first voyage was from Havana, Cuba to Tacoma, Washington, carrying 89,000 bags of sugar. It was during this trip, on May 2, 1944, that the ship went aground off of Gorda Point, Nicaragua. Unable to free the ship, the Captain hailed the freighter, SS Denny, who managed to pull the concrete ship loose after about ten hours work. The crew of the Denny was awarded one half of one month's wages, $1750, as a salvage prize for their efforts. In a report issued about the incident, the crew's "promptitude, skill and success" was described as "beyond criticism."

After working in the sugar transport trade for one year, the JOHN SMEATON was delivered by A.H. Bull Steamship Company to the U.S. Army, by order of the War Shipping Administration, on June 8, 1945. The concrete ship, now the U.S.A.T. JOHN SMEATON, was assigned to Seattle where the Army used her as a training ship for teaching stevedoring, winch operation, small boat handling, etc.

The JOHN SMEATON spent one year as an army ship and was delivered back to the War Shipping Administration for lay-up at Olympia, Washington on June 7, 1946. She remained there until the Powell River Company purchased her on December 8, 1947, taking possession on January 28, 1948. The JOHN SMEATON was towed to Powell River and anchored at the end of the breakwater, just north of the ALBERTOLITE.

The Henri Le Chatelier is moved during the 2002/03 breakwater reconfiguration.

John A Campbell

The positions of the breakwater ships changed over time as the requirements of the log pond dictated, and as older hulks were moved out and new ships arrived. While she has been anchored in several spots in the breakwater, the JOHN SMEATON became

known as HULK #4, and occupied the fourth spot from the north end of the breakwater. During the breakwater reconfiguration of 2002, she was pulled in closer to shore to form one side of the new barge storage area, but is still the fourth ship from the north end.

SS Henri Le Chatelier

Henri Le Chatelier was a French industrial chemist perhaps best remembered for "Le Chatelier's principle," which deals with the reaction of systems in equilibrium. He experimented with the chemistry of various types of cement during the late 19th Century, and is considered to be one of the great scientists and teachers of his day.

The SS HENRI LE CHATELIER was floated in her basin on January 30, 1944 along with sister ships JOHN GRANT and L.J. VICAT. Her construction had begun on August 30, 1943. The concrete ship, McCloskey and Company hull #11, underwent her sea trials on July 13,1944. She was documented on July 27, 1944, and turned over to the War Shipping Administration. They contracted her to the A.H. Bull Steamship Company for operation in the sugar trade.

She began her first voyage under the command of Captain Wilbur T. Miller, sailing in ballast to Cuba to load sugar, but put into Edgemont Key, Florida with mechanical problems. Once repairs were made, the HENRI LE CHATELIER was employed all around the Gulf of Mexico, carrying sugar from Cuba to Philadelphia, New Orleans, Mobile, and other ports. She also carried supplies to U.S. Army bases in the Caribbean.

On April 2, 1945 the SS HENRI LE CHATELIER was involved in a collision and returned to Tampa, where she became embroiled in a dispute between the War Shipping Administration and McCloskey and Company over the terms of the builder's guarantees. An estimated $58,000 was required to repair cracks that had formed, causing leaks from the ship's fuel tanks through her sides and bulkheads. Another $10,000 was needed for repairs to damage caused in the collision. The Maritime Commission eventually settled with McCloskey and approved the repairs. On June 25, 1945, A.H. Bull Steamship Company withdrew the ship from service and handed her over to the U.S. Army.

The U.S.A.T. HENRI LE CHATELIER served with the Army for a few months, arriving at Los Angeles on September 6, 1945 and was delivered to the War Shipping Administration for lay-up at the Suisan Bay, California Reserve yard on November 2, 1945. She remained at Suisan Bay until she was sold to the Powell River Company on December 8, 1947. The company took possession of the ship on February 12, 1948 and she was towed to join the breakwater.

The HENRI LE CHATELIER was the first ship to be placed in the north breakwater. She was later moved to the south breakwater where the hulks of the CHARLESTON and HURON once protected the log pond from the fierce southeasters. Known as Hulk #9, she was the second vessel from the rock breakwater. With the reconfiguration of the breakwater in 2002/2003, the HENRI LE CHATELIER has been moved

Henri Le Chatelier shows damage to her stern from collision with the Quartz during a storm.

John A Campbell

in closer to shore and is the sixth ship from the breakwater's north end.

SS L.J. Vicat

Louis Vicat was a French civil engineer who researched the properties of hydraulic limes and cements

Another view of the Henri Le Chatelier, highlighting the damage to her stern.

John A Campbell

The Armand Considere before her deck housing was removed. The box-like structure on her deck was used to house Japanese prisoners.

NorskeCanada Millennium Project

tracted by the War Shipping Administration for operation by Lykes Brothers for use in the sugar trade. The L.J. VICAT sailed the Gulf of Mexico, visiting many of the major ports in the region until November. While leaving port at Mobile, Alabama the concrete merchant ship lost her rudder and collided with a dock, causing and receiving considerable damage. She was taken back to the Hooker's Point yard at Tampa under the tow of two tugs, and was repaired before returning to her duties as a sugar carrier.

In June 1945, the SS L.J. VICAT was withdrawn from service by Lykes Brothers and was handed over to the U.S. Army at New Orleans. She was

for the construction of bridges and roads during the early 19th Century. The construction of the concrete steamship, L.J. VICAT was started on August 18, 1942. She was launched with her sisters, HENRI LE CHATELIER and JOHN GRANT on January 30, 1944 and was McCloskey and Company hull #12.

She was documented on July 27, 1944 and was con-

to be assigned to the South Pacific, but was never to see this duty. Merchant seaman Andrew Bozard remembered:

When I went aboard the VICAT I was fresh out of maritime school at St. Petersburg, Florida. That ship looked like it had never been cleaned

The breakwater before the last reconfiguration. Broadside in the foreground are the Armand Considere, L.J. Vicat, Thaddeus Merriman, and John Smeaton.

John A Campbell

up or painted. We had a good many men from the USMSTS. These men cleaned and painted the VICAT, it looked new when we finished. We were all very proud of her. We were anchored right in the crescent of the Mississippi River for a few weeks while they installed refrigeration in one of the cargo holds by a contractor. When the work was finished, we started out to the New Orleans Port of Embarkation where the VICAT got out of control as we approached the docking area. That is when the VICAT hit the Liberty Ship. This was sometime in July 1945.

We had two tugs helping us, but were also under our own power. I don't know for sure what caused the collision, it was about seven A.M. I was having breakfast when we collided, at first it was only a sort of jolt. I stood up and that is when we hit the wharf. I was thrown across the room and hit the wall and knocked unconscious for a few minutes. I still suffer at times from the neck injury I sustained at that time. The VICAT had a large hole in the hull and damage all the way down to the bottom of the hull, I don't know how it could be repaired. I was just seventeen years old at that time. I am now seventy-four. That is the way I remember it, but I can't be sure what happened to the VICAT after I left.

Damage to both the Liberty ship and the L.J. VICAT was serious, and the concrete ship was returned to Tampa for repairs. When her repairs were completed, she was assigned to the West Coast. She arrived at Los Angeles around the time of the Japanese surrender.

With the end of the war, the L.J. VICAT was decommissioned and laid up at the Suisan Bay Reserve yard. The Powell River Company was awarded sale of the ship on December 8, 1947 and she left Suisan Bay on February 17 under tow of the tug AGNES FOSS. Upon her arrival at Powell River, the L.J. VICAT became the third vessel in the north breakwater, anchored behind the ARMAND CONSIDERE. Today she is known as Hulk #2 and is the second ship from the breakwater's north end.

U.S.A.T. Armand Considere

Armand Considere, a French civil engineer, was a pioneer in the use of reinforced concrete to support long spans. The concrete steamship ARMAND CONSIDERE, McCloskey and Company hull #16, was floated in her basin in late May of 1944 with her sis-

ters FRANCOIS HENNEBIQUE and P.M. ANDERSON. This was the sixth group of ships to be launched at Hooker's Point. Unlike the previous ships launched at Tampa, these three vessels never had a private operator and were delivered in September 1944 directly to the U.S. Army for use in the South Pacific as storeships.

The U.S. Army used the storeships as floating warehouses. It is a little-known fact that during World War II, the U.S. Army operated a larger fleet of ships and boats than did the U.S. Navy. Compared to the Navy's 74,708 vessels, the Army had 111,000. In cargo carrying, the Army also outdid the Navy, with a total dead-weight capacity of 17.3 million tons of dry cargo and passenger ships compared to 8 million tons for Naval ships.

The island-hopping nature of the Pacific war dictated that the Americans had to carry all of their supplies with them. The storeships were moved in to advanced bases. Faster cargo vessels from the U.S. unloaded their payloads onto the storeships, and then returned home to reload. Supplies were then distributed from the concrete ships to the troops as needed. These vessels, along with the Maritime Commission barges that saw similar service, became well known in the South Pacific as the "Crockery Ships."

The ARMAND CONSIDERE served as a "Crockery Ship" at Pacific bases for the duration of the war. Toward the end of the war, a large wooden house was built on her deck. This block-like structure was fitted with accommodations for Japanese prisoners of war and the concrete ship became a holding and transport ship for POWs. At the end of the war, the ship made at least one voyage to Japan, repatriating captured Japanese soldiers at Yokohama.

Upon her return to the United States, the ARMAND CONSIDERE was laid up at Suisan Bay, California. She was awarded for sale to the Powell River Company on December 8, 1947 and in April 1948 was towed to Powell River. She was placed in the north breakwater just behind the HENRI LE CHATELIER. Today, known as Hulk #1, she is the hulk that is closest to the mill, and is the only one of Powell River's McCloskey and Company ships to sport the remains of an olive green army paint job.

SS Thaddeus Merriman

Thaddeus Merriman was an American civil engineer who was involved in the construction of dams in the New York watershed during the 1920s and 1930s. The Merriman Dam, the main dam in the Rondout Reservoir system, was named for him. He was the chief engineer on the project, and he passed away during its construction.

The steamship THADDEUS MERRIMAN, McCloskey and Company hull #23, was launched on September 24, 1944 with sister ships EDWIN CLARENCE ECKEL and EMILE N. VIDAL. This was the last group of concrete ships launched at Hooker's Point, and the launching marked the end of McCloskey and Company's concrete shipbuilding program. She underwent her sea trials on November 25, 1944.

The THADDEUS MERRIMAN was delivered to the War Shipping Administration who then contracted her to the A.H. Bull Steamship Company on November 30, 1944. She sailed around the Gulf of Mexico carrying sugar, fruit, and general cargo. This ship also experienced mechanical problems, having to be towed back to port on at least one occasion after being disabled by engine problems.

The THADDEUS MERRIMAN was withdrawn from service by A.H. Bull and was delivered to the U.S. Army at New Orleans on June 14, 1945. The ship was assigned to the South Pacific for use as a storeship, but she was never to get there. Headed for the Philippines, she lost her rudder while steaming off the west coast of Mexico. The U.S.A.T. THADDEUS MERRIMAN was towed to San Pedro, California arriving there about two days before the Japanese surrender. The ship was allocated to the Burns Steamship Company, who was charged with towing the vessel from San Pedro to San Francisco where she was laid up at the Suisan Bay Reserve Yard.

The Powell River Company was awarded the sale of the THADDEUS MERRIMAN on December 8, 1947, but left her in the custody of the U.S. Maritime Commission until December 15, 1948. The company paid $7960 to store the ship in California for that time. The tug AGNES FOSS towed the concrete ship to an unknown facility, where she was stripped of valuables before being towed to Powell River in 1950. The ship spent some time moored at the mill before being moved into the breakwater. Later she was moved into the spot vacated by the ISLAND CARRIER. Today known as Hulk #3, she lies next in line to the L.J. VICAT.

U.S.A.T. P.M. Anderson

Colonel Peter M. Anderson was an American engineer who was very involved in the First World War concrete shipbuilding program. During the Second World War he returned to concrete shipbuilding. At the time of his death in 1942, he was involved in designing the B7-A1 concrete oil barges for the U.S. Maritime Commission.

The concrete steamship P.M. ANDERSON, McCloskey and Company hull #18, was launched in late May 1944 along with her sister ships ARMAND CONSIDERE and FRANCOIS HENNEBIQUE. She was delivered to the U.S. Army on September 30, 1944. Her wartime service consisted of duty around the Philippines as a transport and storeship. On her return trip to the United Sates after the war's end, she left Manila and journeyed to Honolulu. She left the Hawaiian Islands on June 21, 1946, bound for Mobile, Alabama.

On June 30, nine days out of Honolulu, the third officer reported to the ship's master, Roko M. Kohn, that the ship had failed to respond to the wheel and was yawing excessively. The seas were heavy, with force 5 winds, and swift action was taken to ensure the safety of the ship. Inspection of the steering engine showed no problems, but when the chief engineer inspected the rudder from a bosun's chair, all he found was the stub of the rudder post, the rudder having sheared off.

The radio operator advised Honolulu of the ship's situation and Navy tug ATA 207 was dispatched to tow the vessel to San Diego. While they were waiting for the tug's arrival, the crew cut the forward starboard life raft loose and towed it as a sea anchor, trying to keep the ship turned into the wind and waves.

On July 2 radio communication was established with the tug. The next day, after firing rockets and sweeping the sky with the ship's searchlight, the tug found the crippled steamship and took her under tow. Seventeen days later the P.M. ANDERSON arrived at San Pedro, California, after an eventful tow, which included broken tow lines, mechanical breakdowns of the tug and mixed weather. The voyage was uncomfortable and the ship yawed heavily while being towed.

The concrete ship was transferred to the Suisan Bay Reserve yard a few days after arriving at San Pedro. She was laid up there until she was purchased by the Powell River Company in February 1956 for a total price of $34,042 including duty, taxes, towing and repairs. In preparation for the move to Powell River, the ship was moved to a dock where she was stripped of all equipment and metal parts.

In August 1956, the P.M. ANDERSON was taken under tow by the Kingcome Navigation tug N.R. LANG for the journey to Powell River. As she was being towed north, the tug crew noticed the ship starting to list and squat down at the stern. She was towed into Coos Bay, Oregon as the problem worsened and the ship sank into the shallows of the harbour. The vessel was pumped out and refloated. Concrete blocks were poured over her rudderpost and propeller shaft stuffing box to seal them before her journey was continued.

When she arrived at Powell River, the P.M. ANDERSON was moored at the mill for a short time before being moved up the coast to the Powell River Company's booming ground at Teakerne Arm for use as a breakwater. Here the concrete ship remained until 1961. At that time she was moved back to the mill to join her sister ships in the breakwater. Known as Hulk #7, she was the second ship to the south of the gap in the breakwater. During the 2002 reconfiguration, the P.M. ANDERSON was moved closer to shore and is the fifth ship from the breakwater's north end.

SS Emile N. Vidal

Emile N. Vidal was an American engineer who was concerned with experimentation and development of concrete mixes and products. He co-authored numerous papers on the subject and was involved in several of the "New Deal" projects in the U.S. during the depression years, including the Hoover Dam.

The concrete steamship, EMILE N. VIDAL was launched on September 24, 1944, along with her sister ships EDWIN CLARENCE ECKEL and THADDEUS MERRIMAN. She was McCloskey and Company hull #24, the last of the Second World War concrete steamships. On December 2, 1944 the ship underwent her sea trials and was delivered by McCloskey and Company to the War Shipping Administration on December 9. She was immediately contracted to Agwilines Inc. for operation in the Gulf sugar trade.

The EMILE N. VIDAL's career had an unlucky beginning. On December 12, 1944 she was moored alongside

The P.M. Anderson moored at the mill before her move to Teakerne Arm.

the SS JOHN GRANT, another of the McCloskey and Company vessels. When she shifted at her moorings, she sideswiped the other ship, causing $700 in damage. After she was repaired, the EMILE N. VIDAL went into the merchant trade around the Gulf of Mexico and Caribbean.

She was delivered to the U.S. Army on May 26, 1945 at the Port of New Orleans where she was cleaned up and received $4500 in repairs. The concrete steamship was assigned to the South Pacific, where she operated around the Philippines as a transport and storeship. Following the Japanese surrender the U.S.A.T. EMILE N. VIDAL sailed from Leyte in the Philippines on November 7, 1945 carrying 7,207,982 pounds of army surplus rations for use as post war relief supplies in China. She arrived in Shanghai on

November 19 where the rations were unloaded. This was her last working voyage and she was ordered back to the United States. During her homeward trip, the ship lost her propeller and had to be towed to San Francisco. She was subsequently towed to Oregon where she was returned to the U.S. Maritime Commission and laid up in the Astoria Reserve Fleet.

The Powell River Company was awarded sale of the ship on December 8, 1947 and took possession of her on February 11, 1948. They in turn sold her to the Pennsylvania Salt Manufacturing Company (Pennsalt) for $7700. Pennsalt used her as a bulk salt storage hull at their plant at Wilbridge, near Portland, Oregon. The vessel remained at that plant, moored at their dock for almost 20 years, until MacMillan

George Allen Aerial Photos Ltd.

An aerial view of the breakwater from 1961. The hulk of the Cardena can be seen between the hog fuel barges at the north end. Counter-clockwise from there are the Armand Considere, L.J. Vicat, Thaddeus Merriman, John Smeaton, Peralta, P.M. Anderson, Henri Le Chatelier, Quartz and YOGN 82.

Bloedel, the successor of the Powell River Company, purchased her around 1965.

The EMILE N. VIDAL became known as Hulk #5 and was the ship to the north of the breakwater entrance. Her years as a salt storage hull with Pennsalt have left her in poor condition. The deterioration of the concrete, which is limited to the outside of the rest of the breakwater hulks, is also taking place inside the EMILE N. VIDAL's hull. In 1991 the vessel's interior was sprayed with a layer of concrete in an attempt to extend her service life. Despite this, she is in the worst condition of any of Powell River's McCloskey and Company ships, and if any of the Second World War concrete steamships are to be removed from the breakwater in the future, she will surely be the one. In January 2003, the EMILE N. VIDAL was brought in closer to shore and occupies the seventh spot from the north in the reconfigured breakwater. ⚓

8

The Concrete Tanker of World War I

No one in the Shipping Board or the Fleet Corporation ever favored the concrete ship.

… Undoubtedly the fact which greatly encouraged the advocates of concrete construction was the building of the Faith. This concrete vessel was built by private capital in San Francisco. Its completion was heralded as the last word in ship construction.

Edward N. Hurley, Chairman of the United States Shipping Board
The Bridge to France, 1927

Not all of the concrete vessels that form the breakwater were built for use in the Second World War. The last of the First World War 7500 dead weight ton concrete tankers, built for the United States Shipping Board Emergency Fleet Corporation, remains afloat at Powell River.

As mentioned in Chapter 6, W. Leslie Comyn had approached the USSB in 1917 to ask for funding to build concrete hulled vessels. The USSB was still undecided about the viability of vessels built of con-

maiden voyage to Vancouver, BC carrying a cargo of copper ore and salt. Two research engineers from the Emergency Fleet Corporation's Department of Concrete Ship Construction were also aboard to gauge the ship's performance.

The FAITH proved to be a seaworthy and profitable ship for her owners, despite the fact that she suffered from the same disabilities as the concrete vessels that followed her. Due to her experimental construction, the USSB had granted her immunity from their commandeering orders, and she was free

The first American concrete steamship, Faith, at Vancouver in 1918.

Courtesy of Frank A Clapp

crete and turned Comyn down. He returned to California, disappointed but undaunted, and managed to borrow enough money to form the San Francisco Shipbuilding Company in September 1917. He immediately began the construction of the first American concrete steamship, the FAITH.

Comyn built the FAITH at Redwood City, California using a crew of 150 men. She was built in 73 days and cost $750,000. Many dignitaries, including Rudolph Wig, the Chief Engineer of the Emergency Fleet Corporation's Concrete Ship Section, attended her launching on March 14, 1918. She was commissioned on May 13, 1918 and nine days later sailed on her

to sail to friendly ports around the world benefiting from the high shipping rates created by the war. She became the first concrete ship to cross the Atlantic Ocean, the first to traverse the Panama Canal, and sail the Mediterranean. She carried more cargo to more ports than any other concrete ship that came after her. Nonetheless, the glut of more efficient steel ships that became available after the armistice rendered her obsolete. She ended up being stripped of her equipment in December 1921, and was towed to Cuba for use as a breakwater.

At the time of her launching, however, the FAITH proved to be a powerful incentive to the USSB to proceed with funding for the concrete shipbuilding program. Enthusiastic reports about her from Rudolph Wig caught the attention of President Woodrow Wilson. With pressure from his office, the directors of the USSB finally agreed to award contracts for the construction of concrete ships.

The San Francisco Shipbuilding Company had already demonstrated that they were quite capable of building ships from concrete, and so, were one of the first companies to be awarded a contract for the construction of eight of the USSB 7500 dead weight ton vessels. The location that was chosen to build Comyn's shipyard was Government Island in the San Antonio Estuary and a 25-year lease for the property was signed with the cities of Oakland and Alameda in California on June 5, 1918. Work began immediately erecting the forms for two of the ships, to be named PALO ALTO and TWILIGHT.

The hulls were made entirely of reinforced concrete, except for the huge cast steel stern frames and the hawse pipes for the anchors. It took approximately 2800 cubic yards of concrete to build each of the hulls. About 600 cubic yards were used for the bottom, up to the turn of the bilge. Another 1200 yards formed the side shells from the bilge, up to and including the second deck. About 800 yards were used from the second deck, up to and including the main deck and 200 yards were used to form the ship's superstructure. The mixed concrete was placed into the forms, tamped to fill the voids, and cured for 10 to 20 days. The ships' names were cast in raised letters on their bows.

For marine service, approximately seven times as much reinforcing steel was used as compared to land

The Peralta's outer hull forms are complete and placement of reinforcing steel is underway, November 19, 1918.

U.S. National Archives and Records Administration

The launch of Peralta, October 26, 1920.

US National Archives and Records Administration

construction, about five per cent of the cross sectional area of the concrete. Structures above the bridge deck and the aft deckhouse were built of wood. Bulkheads for the deckhouses were also built of wood.

Once the hull was completed the forms were removed, and the incomplete ship was launched sideways into the water. The first of the ships, the PALO ALTO was launched on May 29, 1919. The second ship, whose name was changed from TWILIGHT to PERALTA during construction, was launched on October 26, 1920. Work on a third hull, to be named the WALLEMAR and to be a 7500 dead weight ton general cargo ship, was abandoned when the USSB cancelled the contracts on all ships that were not in the late stages of construction.

SS Peralta

After her launching, the PERALTA was moved to the outfitter's dock where the installation of her equipment was completed and she was made ready for service. Like the rest of the 7500 dead weight ton ships built for the USSB, she was 420 feet in length, had a beam of 54 feet, and a depth of 34 feet. She had six tanks for the storage of cargo oil, giving her a capacity of 50,000 barrels. Two wing tanks held fuel for her boilers, and peak tanks and dry storage spaces fore and aft added to her capacity. As tankers go, she would be considered small by today's standards, but in her day she was a sizeable ship.

The PERALTA's three watertube boilers and 2800

horsepower, triple expansion engine were located amidships. Power was transferred to her 11-ton, 15-foot diameter bronze propeller through a 200-foot long, 18-inch diameter steel shaft.

The ship's "three island" hull emulated the other Ferris ships that were built for the USSB. With her plumb stem, central stack, and counter stern, she looked like a larger version of the USSB standard wooden cargo ship. Her two masts carried booms capable of lifting a 5-ton load. The tanker's main deck was provided with bosun's and carpenter's stores foreword. Crew's quarters and a hospital area were located aft. Officer's cabins and a radio room were on the central bridge deck.

The Peralta joined the breakwater in 1961. Some of her original wooden superstructure remained standing until the early 1990s.

NorskeCanada Millennium Project

The PERALTA was documented in October 1920 and it was reported that she was sold to the American Fuel Oil and Transportation Co. for $700,000. This sale apparently was never completed. She was reported sold again in December to the Lincoln Steamship Co. of New York for $765,000, but again the sale fell through and the ship remained laid up at San Francisco. In 1924 the concrete tanker that had cost nearly $1.5 million to build was sold to the Portland Cement Company for $12,500.

The Portland Cement Company stripped the PERALTA of her equipment and sold the hull. She was then outfitted as a fish reduction plant for making fertiliser, and was towed to Alaska where she operated for several years in Bristol Bay. Around 1932, now owned by a shipyard, she was returned to California where Elwyn C. Hale purchased her and fitted her with more fish-handling equipment. She was moved to Richmond, California where she was used to process sardines.

In 1945 much of the California sardine fishery was shut down when the sardines disappeared. The PERALTA was eventually moved to an anchorage at Antioch, California in 1948. Hale had her fish-handling

equipment removed and on October 14, 1958 donated the ship to the Presbytery of San Francisco.

In early 1961 the hulks of the CHARLESTON and HURON were nearing the end of their service life. The hulls had developed leaks that had been repaired, but the old cruisers were obviously on their last legs. MacMillan, Bloedel, and Powell River Limited began looking for vessels that would allow them to remove the old warships from the breakwater.

Initially, they placed a bid on a surplus concrete pontoon from a floating bridge project at Seattle, Washington. The pontoon, 360 feet long and 50 feet wide, was about the same size as the concrete ships already in the breakwater, but another organisation outbid the company for its purchase. Having failed to obtain the pontoon, the company was given the opportunity to purchase the PERALTA in California for a price of $21,000. With additional fees for duty, inspection, repairs to ready the old tanker for the long tow to Powell River and a towing bill of $13,825, the total cost added up to $56,999.73. The Kingcome Navigation tug N.R. LANG took a week to tow the ship to the breakwater.

The PERALTA was placed in the breakwater at the south end of the log pond entrance. She remained there for four decades. Her hull, which has been afloat for more than 80 years, has deteriorated badly. She was almost lost during the 1960s, when late one night she was noticed to be sitting lower in the water than normal. By the time that pumps and men had been mobilised, the waves were lapping at her hatch coamings. With every available pump working to capacity, the ship finally began to reverse her descent. Holes in her hull were patched, and she resumed her guard duty on the log pond.

In 1968, in an attempt to extend the life of the PERALTA, a contractor who built and repaired swimming pools applied a spray-on concrete mix to her thinning hull. This material has started to slough off. The PERALTA is the oldest and is in the poorest condition of any of the breakwater ships and it is probable that the old tanker's days are numbered. Since 1961, she has been known as Hulk # 6, but now has been moved in closer to shore and is the ninth ship from the north end of the breakwater. ⚓

Peralta in March 2003, the oldest concrete ship still afloat in the world.

John A Campbell

9

The Concrete Barges

… Late spring of 1944 saw the first of the "crockery" ships come into Majuro. They were the Trefoil and the Quartz, large concrete barges with power plants for refrigeration, lighting, and windlass, but not for motive power.

… The disadvantage of the barges was their need of powerful towing vessels when a major move was undertaken; but in a critical period of the war they furnished facilities and services which otherwise could not have been provided. In addition to the 13 for provisions and supplies, there were others of similar hull design for the bulk storage of fuel oil and gasoline, each holding up to 66,000 barrels."

Rear Admiral Worral Reed Carter
Beans, Bullets, and Black Oil

he last two ships in the breakwater are of a different sort than the rest. Although they are similar in size and appearance to the rest of the concrete vessels, they are actually two examples of the unpowered reinforced concrete barges that were built for the U.S. Maritime Commission during the Second World War. Both of these vessels were designed for towing, singly or in tandem, by tugs or other ships, and served during World War II with the U.S. Navy.

USS Quartz IX-150

In the spring of 1942, a contract was awarded to Barrett and Hilp of San Francisco for the construction of 26 concrete barges to be used for the transportation of bauxite, the ore used in the production of aluminium. J.F. Barrett and H.H. Hilp had been partners in the firm since 1931, engaging in heavy construction work using concrete. They had been one of the prime contractors during the construction of the Golden Gate Bridge. They built the approach piers and anchorages, and worked on the pavement for the spans and approaches.

Barrett and Hilp built Belair Shipyards at the mouth of Colma Creek, utilising six graving docks for the construction and launch of the barges. Like the Hookers Point yard of McCloskey and Company, women formed a large part of the workforce and were found to be excellent welders.

The placing of concrete for the first of the barges began on December 7, 1942. The vessel was launched on June 16, 1943. Like most of these vessels, designated B7-D1 by the U.S. Maritime Commission, she was named for a mineral, AGATE.

The B7-D1 barges were 366 feet in length overall. They had a beam of 54 feet and a depth of 35 feet. They displaced 10,970 tons with a dead weight of 5,687 tons. Three Cummins Diesel powered generators provided electrical power for lighting, pumps, steering gear, etc. Each of the vessels cost approximately $1.5 million to build.

The Maritime Commission designation for barges, as it was for ships, was a description of the characteristics of the vessels. The letter "B" indicated that the vessel was a barge, having no means of propulsion. The number "7" was an indication of length, in this case a barge between 350 and 400 feet long. "D1" was the letter and number combination that applied to the hull design and modifications.

The six graving docks at Barrett and Hilp's Belair shipyards,, February 1943.

(Top) Builder's hull No. 1, the Agate, passes under the San Francisco-Oakland Bay Bridge.

(Bottom) Five B7-D1 barges at the outfitting wharves in various stages of completion. The Barite, sitting low in the water, is undergoing hydrostatic testing. The barge at right has been painted, outfitted and is ready for delivery.

US National Archives and Records Administration

Action on the deck of the Quartz at a Pacific atoll during WW II. Tracked cranes were used to raise material from the below-decks warehouse area.

US National Archives and Records Administration

Before long, self-propelled steel ships became available to carry bauxite. The Maritime Commission cancelled the contract for six of the 26 barges and the rest were transferred to the military. Of the 20 barges built, 13 were used by the U.S. Navy in the South Pacific as floating warehouses. The U.S. Army operated four others in the same duty.

The twelfth of the B7-D1 barges was built with the name ASHPHALT, but was renamed QUARTZ before launching on December 4, 1943. The barge was completed and was sold to the U.S. Navy on February 10, 1944. She was handed over for service on April 13, 1944. Assigned for duty with the Pacific Fleet, she was towed from San Francisco to Pearl Harbor, arriving on May 10. The QUARTZ was given the Navy designation IX-150, IX indicating a miscellaneous or unclassified vessel.

The QUARTZ was attached to Service Squadrons 8, 9, and 10 and served as a "Crockery Ship" with Lieutenant Commander Paul Runyon in command. The barges were also nicknamed the "Green Dragons," owing to the olive green colour that they were painted, and because of the way that the concrete hulls soaked up the tropical heat during the day and radiated it all night. The heat made staying aboard these ships much like sleeping in a sauna.

A crew of about 55 men operated the navy's B7-D1 barges with 3 officers in charge. Like the McCloskey and Company C1-S-D1 concrete steamships did with the Army, the barges provided stores to the Navy at advanced bases.

Supplied by fast cargo ships from the US, the "Green Dragons" allowed the storage and issue of large amounts of dry goods, general stores, medical supplies, mechanical parts, etc. Often, more than 7000 items were carried aboard, and the vessels served as many as 600 ships in a month. The barges were

USS Quartz IX 150 in the South Pacific during WW II.

US National Archives and Records Administration

also able to take surplus goods from ships that had been reassigned to duties outside of the forward bases. These goods might have otherwise been transported back to the US. The QUARTZ served at Guam, Eniwetok, Leyte, Majuro, and Ulithi, and while she carried many types of supplies, she specialised

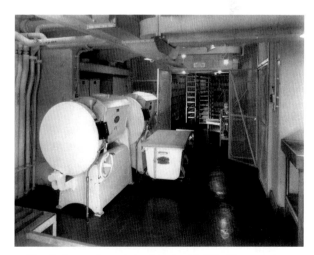

The bakery aboard the Lignite IX 162. The services provided by the Green Dragons were invaluable to the American war effort.

US National Archives and Records Administration

in the handling of clothing.

For handling cargo, mobile cranes on caterpillar tracks were provided. The below deck spaces on the "Green Dragons" were set up much like a shore based warehouse, with areas partitioned off using wood walls and chain link fencing, some being fitted with shelves for smaller items. Stores to be issued were assembled below the deck hatches and lifted out in cargo nets using the deck cranes.

The Quartz at Powell River, November 12, 1956.

NorskeCanada Millennium Project

Several of the barges were equipped with large bakeries or butcher shops, and had substantial refrigerated space in their holds. This allowed the crews of the small boats and patrol vessels that operated with the Service Squadrons to enjoy as good a diet and as many luxuries as the crews of large warships.

The Service Squadrons formed what were essentially huge, mobile naval bases. Stationed in an area close to the battle zone, the "Green Dragons" provided warehouse space and distributed their stock as needed. Other types of vessels in the squadron served as floating hotels, hospital ships, repair ships, fuel storage tankers, fresh water distilleries, ammunition ships, and any other service considered necessary to keep the fleet and armed forces supplied and operating. Floating dry-docks and cranes allowed repairs to ships that were damaged in action. One well-known and popular vessel, a Maritime Commission B5-BJ2 concrete barge, was equipped to manufacture ice cream and could produce ten gallons of the treat every seven seconds.

The proximity of the service groups to the fighting made them convenient targets for Japanese aircraft. For protection, the QUARTZ was fitted with four 20-mm anti-aircraft guns. These were mounted in three gun tubs on metal stands, one large one over the poop deck mounting two guns, and two smaller ones, port and starboard foreword, with one gun each. A twin 40-mm gun was fitted in a circular gun mount above the afterdeck.

John R. Partin, a navy signalman, recalled his experiences as a member of a "Green Dragon's" crew.

I was assigned to the USS CARMITA, IX 152. It was really a concrete barge, green in color and had no propulsion system. It had to hitch a tow from other vessels. It was said to be experimental. Not a ship that one would point to with pride, however it did prove to be very instrumental in supplies for the fleet.

It was attached to ComSerRon 10, along with many other vessels to serve the fleet. We joined the group in Eniwetok and were there for some time. They did a good service because the war had advanced out of supply range. The purpose of this group was to be in the advanced area. Other ships would off load on us and we were stationed there to distribute supplies.

As the war advanced, we were towed to Ulithi. That was some seventy-five miles from Yap, an island that was by-passed in the Caroline Group. The Japanese were still there and caused all the trouble they could. They would patch up a plane and come visit us once in a while. I have watched planes take off to meet them and seen them shot down

We were there and saw the fleet come in from the battle of Leyte. It was really beat up. One

The Test Baker blast at Bikini Atoll pushed a dome of water and debris a mile wide into the sky.

US National Archives and Records Administration

(Top Left) The Quartz has her anchors set during the recent breakwater reconfiguration, January 2003.

Courtesy of Tonia Jurbin

(Bottom) The Quartz after the 2002-2003 reconfiguration.

John A Campbell

destroyer even had its bridge blown off and was under its own steam. Some of the men that used cutting torches was sent to various ships to use them to cut out men that had been killed and was still in sections of the ship. They said the stench was terrible.

A body floated into the harbor one day, he had on only his shorts. I could see the marking, J.L. Walsh. Never did know where he came from. The name has stayed with me for over fifty years now.

At the end of the Second World War the QUARTZ was slated for disposal, but ended up being assigned to Joint Task Force 1 in January 1946. As part of Task group 1.8, Service Group, she took part in Operation Crossroads, the first atomic bomb tests at Bikini Atoll. Here she continued her duties as a "Crockery Ship", providing supplies for the task force in the company of her sister ship, the LIMESTONE IX-158.

There were three tests scheduled to take place at Bikini Atoll, codenamed Test Able, Test Baker, and Test Charlie. The tests were intended to gauge the impact of an atomic attack on naval vessels and a fleet of surplus U.S. vessels and captured Japanese and German ships was assembled in the lagoon. The Able test was an air burst bomb that was exploded 520 feet above the fleet of 95 ships. The damage done by this test was somewhat disappointing, resulting in the sinking of only five of the target vessels. The second explosion, Test Baker, was much more effective.

The Baker bomb was suspended in the water 90 feet below the surface. In one second the bomb pushed a dome of

water and debris, about one mile wide, into the sky. When the millions of tons of material lifted by the detonation collapsed back into the lagoon, it created a wall of radioactive mist and spray that expanded outward at 60 miles per hour. The whole target fleet and much of the support fleet and their crews were contaminated by radiation. As entertainer Bob Hope

(Top) YOGN 82 arrives at Powell River, June 1, 1961.

NorskeCanada Millennium Project

(Bottom) YOGN 82 in the breakwater, April 2002.

John A Campbell

quipped, "As soon as the war ended, we located the one spot on earth that hadn't been touched by war and blew it to hell." Test Charlie was cancelled due to concerns raised during the previous two tests.

Kenneth H. Tripke was a crewman aboard the QUARTZ during the Operation Crossroads tests at Bikini. He was severely affected by the exposure to radiation he received. "I personally was so sick with diarrhea and vomiting for days, I went from 128 to 70-some pounds. I turned a funny colour, lost all my hair on my body." Tripke was treated aboard a hospital ship and fed intravenously. While he survived his brush with radiation sickness, he suffered from health problems for the rest of his life.

After the tests at Bikini in July 1946, the QUARTZ was towed to Kwajalein Atoll where she was declared to be free of contamination. She was towed to Pearl Harbor and then to Bremerton, Washington where she was taken out of service on December 31, 1946. The barge was removed from the Navy Lists on January 22, 1947 and was sold to Foss Launch and Tug Company of Seattle for $7023 on August 11 of that year. They took possession of the vessel on October 23 at Nordland, Washington.

The QUARTZ remained the property of the Foss Company for several years. She was purchased by the Powell River Company for $36,500, and arrived at Powell River on November 12, 1956. After a brief period of time moored in the log pond, the barge was moved to join the P.M. ANDERSON for breakwater use at the company's booming ground at Teakerne Arm. She was towed back to Powell River in 1961 to take her place in the mill's breakwater.

The QUARTZ is easily identifiable by her raised gun mounts, fading green paint, and by the boldly painted name on the side of her hull. She became known as Hulk #8 and was the centre vessel in the southern group of breakwater ships. She has now been moved in closer to shore and is still the eighth ship from the north end of the breakwater.

USS YOGN 82

Early in the U.S. involvement in World War Two it became evident that some method of transporting petroleum products from the Gulf States to the Eastern U.S. would be necessary. To meet this need a fleet of reinforced concrete tanker barges was envisioned. In November 1941 the U.S. Maritime Commission awarded contracts to three shipyards for the construction of 15 of these vessels, with the intention that a total of 50 barges would be built in the first six

months of 1942.

Concrete Ship Constructors was one of the companies that was given a contract. They leased 1 ¼ square miles of tidal lands at National City, California to build their shipyard. Two graving docks, 450 feet long, 75 feet wide, and 30 feet deep were excavated and lined with wood sheet piling. A section of sheet steel piling that could be removed with a crane when launching a barge served to close the basin off from the sea.

The U.S. Maritime Commission had originally designed the barges to operate without a crew, but the maritime authorities decided that each vessel would have to be manned to prevent it from becoming a hazard to navigation in the event of an accident. The barges, modified with safety and defence features, and provided with accommodations for a crew, were designated as U.S. Maritime commission type B7-A2.

The B7-A2 barges were 375 feet in length overall, had a beam of 56 feet, and a depth of 38 feet. Quarters for 12 crew were provided in a deckhouse aft. A small deckhouse amidships housed two 45-horsepower engines that provided power for pumps, winches, lighting and the barge's steering gear. A raised catwalk, running fore and aft from the amidships engine house, gave access to piping, valves and the raised fore and afterdecks.

The first of the B7-A2 barges, named CONCRETE No.1, was launched on October 13, 1942 after 166 days of construction. This was the first launching of an American concrete ship in 20 years. She was completed and delivered to the U.S. Navy on April 13, 1943, 349 days after her construction began. With the details of building these vessels resolved, production rates increased considerably and a total of 22 of the barges were built.

By the time the first barges were launched, their original function had been made redundant by the construction of a pipeline, and the U.S. Navy took over and operated all of the vessels. The sixteenth of the B7-A2 barges to be launched went into service as YOG 82.

Vessels of this type were not considered significant enough by the Navy to be named. Instead, they were given letters and numbers to describe their function and to identify them. In this case, the letters "YO" identify the vessel as a district or yard oiler. The letter "G" indicates that the barge was used to hold gasoline. YOG 82 was essentially a huge floating gasoline station. After the war, the letter "N" was added to the vessel's designation to indicate that she was not self-propelled.

The type of service provided by this class of vessel was much the same as that of other concrete "Crockery Ships." They were usually attached to the Service Squadrons, providing fuel storage capacity, pumping facilities and transport capability at advanced bases, being refilled by tankers from the US. They could also be towed to sea where ships could be refuelled. While this might seem to be the unromantic and mundane side of naval service, these vessels were essential to the American war effort in the Pacific. The military machine runs on fossil fuels, and vessels like YOGN 82 were often the only fuel storage facilities available at Pacific bases. This fact was not lost on the Japanese, who sank three of these vessels, YOG 41, YOG 42 and YO 159. YOG 82 served in the South Pacific with the Service Squadrons at advanced bases such as Eniwetok Lagoon.

B7-A2 barges also served during the Operation Crossroads atomic tests at Bikini Atoll. However, rather than serve as supply ships, two of the concrete vessels served as targets. As an experiment to gauge the effect of an atomic blast on concrete structures, YO 160 and YOG 83 were fitted with sensors and anchored in the target zone. YO 160 was damaged by the Test Able blast, but did not sink. During the Test Baker explosion, the tanker barge was swamped and sank in 140 feet of water. YOG 83 survived the blasts but was later beached and then scuttled at Kwajalein Atoll. The wrecks of abandoned B7-A2 barges still exist in the South Pacific, grounded on beaches where they were left after their usefulness was over.

YOGN 82 was purchased in 1960 by MacMillan, Bloedel, and Powell River Limited for use in the breakwater. A total of $46,500 was paid for the ship, towing, permits, and duty. The Foss Tug and Launch Company towed her to Powell River from Pearl Harbor, arriving on June 1, 1961.

Today, YOGN 82 can be easily identified by the collapsing catwalk that runs between her raised fore and poop decks. She became known as Hulk #10, and is the hulk that is closest to the rock breakwater, the spot vacated by the old CHARLESTON when she was towed off to Kelsey Bay. With the breakwater reconfiguration of 2002, YOGN 82 has been moved in closer to shore and acts as an extension of the rock breakwater. ⚓

An aerial view of the breakwater during the reconfiguration in January 2003. From the mill, the ships are the Armand Considere, L.J. Vicat, Thaddeus Merriman, John Smeaton, P.M. Anderson, Henri Le Chatelier, Emile N. Vidal and the Quartz, which has just been moved. The Peralta, still in her original position, was moved in next to the Quartz. YOGN 82 was moved slightly closer to shore.

Courtesy of Tonia Jurbin

Into the future?

What will the future be for The Hulks at Powell River? They have become the victims of downsizing for the first time and it is possible that some of the ships may eventually be removed from the breakwater. The mill's waterfront still needs to be protected, however, and some of the ships will be staying for the foreseeable future.

A survey of the hulls of seven of the vessels was undertaken in the autumn of 2002. The ships that were surveyed were selected as "keepers," assuming that their appearance had a bearing on their condition. The ships were the ARMAND CONSIDERE, L.J. VICAT, THADDEUS MERRIMAN, JOHN SMEATON, and

can concrete shipbuilding: the old PERALTA, the last of the First World War 7500-dead weight ton tankers and the oldest concrete ship still afloat; the QUARTZ, former Green Dragon and atomic survivor; YOGN 82, concrete tanker barge and veteran of the war in the Pacific; and the crockery ships built by McCloskey and Company, dawdling ships that sailed the Gulf of Mexico in the sugar trade and crossed the Atlantic and Pacific in the service of their country — a collection of vessels unique in the world.

While it will be sad to see the loss of any of Powell River's breakwater ships, the 70-plus year history of the Hulks is one of arrivals and departures. Hope-

The hulks after the 2002/03 reconfiguration. From the foreground Armand Considere, LJ Vicat, Thaddeus Merriman, John Smeaton, PM Anderson, Henri Le Chatelier, Emile N Vidal, Quartz, Peralta and YOGN 82.

John A Campbell

P.M. ANDERSON. The YOGN 82 was surveyed as a fall-back, in case one of the others was found to be in too poor condition to consider keeping. Surprisingly, the survey has given them a service life of another 10 to 20 years, assuming no major repairs are done. Reconditioning the ships will extend that life span to 25 years or more.

The Hulks represent a veritable museum of Ameri-

fully, the final departure will not come for many years.

The success of the floating breakwater at the Powell River mill has given it one of the longest life spans of any of British Columbia's ship breakwaters, but not all of these attempts to master the forces of nature succeeds as effectively. Only a few miles from the mill, Powell River's other ship breakwater is largely forgotten. ⚓

10

The Wolfson Creek Breakwater

Familiar sights along the BC coast are the numerous old hulks that have been piled up to make breakwaters. Casual observers usually think of shipwrecks and barratry, but actually the hulks were beached for a purpose.

Norm Hacking, "On the Waterfront"
The Vancouver Province, 1955

A few miles south of Powell River, the estuary of Wolfson (Lang) Creek has been the waterfront terminus for logging operations since the late 1800s. Several logging railways, and later, truck logging outfits worked from the camp built at the western end of Lang Bay. A wharf and log dump was built on the eastern side of the creek's mouth, and was extended with wood pilings to form a breakwater. However, the storms that occasionally roll up Malaspina Strait from the southeast, combined with high tides, could still agitate the water in the log pond causing booms to break up.

In the early 1950s, Mahood Logging Limited took over the site, under the direction of Ernie Mahood. Mahood was no stranger to the concept of ship breakwaters. He had moved his operation from Oyster Bay near Campbell River in 1952. The Oyster Bay booming ground was formed by a number of old ships' hulks that had been grounded in shallow water.

Determined to improve the Wolfson Creek log pond's protection, he began an unsuccessful attempt to use derelict ships to extend the breakwater.

SS Capilano II

The first ship that was purchased by Mahood was the former Union Steamship, CAPILANO II. The CAPILANO was built by BC Marine Ltd. of Vancouver and was launched on December 20, 1919. She was 135 feet long, 26 feet, 9 inches in beam, had a draft of 8 feet, 2 inches, and was of 374 gross tons. Her hull was built of Douglas Fir.

The CAPILANO's engine was a second-hand triple expansion machine that had been removed from the steamship, WASHINGTON. It produced 51 net horsepower and could drive the ship to 13 knots. She had a cargo capacity of 50 tons and was licensed to carry 350 passengers from May to September, 150 passengers in the winter.

The Union Steamship Capilano II.

Vancouver Maritime Museum

The Union Steamship Company had initially intended the ship for use in servicing their resort at Selma Park, with additional scheduled trips to Roberts Creek, Wilson Creek, Halfmoon Bay, and Buccaneer Bay. She was also used on the Bowen Island to Squamish run up Howe Sound, as well as excursions farther up the coast. The CAPILANO went into

The CAPILANO's final voyage as a Union Steamship took place on January 31, 1949. Under the command of Captain Robert Naughty, she was scheduled to steam up the Sunshine Coast to Stillwater, a destination that was very close to her final resting-place. A gale force westerly wind was blowing as the ship left Vancouver harbour carrying six passengers. After

The Bedwell (Capilano) extends the Wolfson Creek Breakwater.

Powell River Historical Museum

this service on May 1, 1920, beginning a three-decade long career.

The CAPILANO did not share in the misfortunes of her larger Union Steamship sister, CARDENA. She was reported to have run aground only once in her history, running up on the mud flats at McNab Creek but managing to back herself off without difficulty. The biggest problem that was experienced during the ship's service was with an unruly steering chain that could jam the helm, rendering her uncontrollable. This persistent problem had dire consequences in February 1947. While steaming to Hopkins Landing under the command of Captain Jock Malcolmson, the helm jammed. This upset the captain so much that he yelled, "Oh my God!" and collapsed in the wheelhouse. The mate took command of the ship and, after having repaired the steering, took her into Gibsons Landing. A doctor pronounced Captain Malcolmson dead at 55 years of age.

more than two hours of pounding into the storm, the crew reported that the forecastle decking was leaking and working loose. Closer inspection revealed that the little ship was coming apart at the seams. Captain Naughty managed to put into Gibsons Landing, where the passengers were put on buses to their destinations. When the insurance adjusters inspected the CAPILANO the next day, it was clear that her career was over and she was condemned on the spot.

The CAPILANO was sold to the Canadian Fishing Company Limited of Vancouver on June 27, 1949, at which time she was stripped and converted to a barge. On August 24, 1951 the former Union Steamer was renamed BEDWELL. In December 1952, BEDWELL was sold to David Yackbowitz of Vancouver, presumably for scrapping. In 1953, Mahood bought the stripped hull and beached her at the end of the piling breakwater at Wolfson Creek.

The arrival of the BEDWELL marked the beginning

of Mahood's problems with his breakwater. After a few good south-easterly gales, the hulk slipped away from the pilings down into the log pond, interfering with boat traffic and the movement of booms. Finally, a bulldozer was brought down to the beach at low tide and the ship was broken up where she lay.

Charles R. Wilson

Mahood purchased a second vessel after the hulk of the CAPILANO was beached at Wolfson Creek. As the old Union Steamship was pushed down the slope of the beach by the wind and waves, the former fishing schooner CHARLES R. WILSON was beached above her to slow her descent and to continue to protect the log pond.

The three-masted schooner Charles R. Wilson anchored on Lake Union.

Washington State University Historical Photo Collection.

Hans Bendixsen built the CHARLES R. WILSON at Fairhaven, California in 1891, a three-masted schooner 150 feet in length, and of 328 gross tons. She was designed to be a lumber carrier and worked as such until the Pacific Coast Codfish Company of Seattle purchased her in 1913. She was converted for use in the Bering Sea fishery with the addition of quarters for 35 or more crew, and enlargement of her

galley and mess. The lumber schooner's steam donkey was removed and replaced with a single cylinder 12-horsepower gasoline engine. This was used to drive the ship's anchor windlass and deck winch for raising sails, hoisting dories, and any other heavy lifting jobs.

The West Coast cod fishery was similar in technique and equipment to that of the East Coast. Many of the men employed in the fishery were experienced eastern dorymen who had moved west. The schooners would sail from their homeport to the fishing grounds. Once there, each fisherman would row his dory to the area that he wanted to fish, often a mile from the ship. Once in place, the fisherman would anchor and drop several fishing lines, each with a number of baited hooks, over the side. When the time came to retrieve the lines, the fisherman hauled them in by hand, coiling the lines at his feet. Any fish that were brought in would have their throats cut to bleed them and were then tossed into the bottom of the dory. The lines were then rebaited and put back over the side. Once the dory was full of cod, sometimes almost to the point of being swamped, the fisherman rowed back to the schooner.

Back at the ship, the cod were unloaded from the dory, cleaned and split and salted to preserve them. The dories were hoisted onto the schooner's deck and cleaned out. To store the dories the thwarts were removed and five or six would be nested together, saving room on deck. A fisherman's day started at about 4:30 AM. Usually the dories were hauled out around 5:00 or 6:00 in the evening. Fishing took place seven days a week while on the fishing grounds.

The main difference between the East and West Coast fisheries was the distance travelled to fish.

Operating out of Seattle, the CHARLES R. WILSON was out of port for at least five months on each voyage to the Bering Sea. The schooner did not put into port to resupply while she was away, and so she had to carry all of the supplies needed to fish, and enough food for the duration of the voyage. She was equipped with 16 dories and carried 350 tons of salt for curing the cod.

In 1928 the first powered dories came into use in the cod fishery. A well was built into the bottom of the dory into which an outboard motor could be

The Charles R. Wilson and Capilano were soon washed into the booming ground entrance.

Powell River Historical Museum

mounted. This greatly reduced the time and effort required by the fishermen in rowing to and from their fishing areas and left more time for fishing. The powered dories could not be nested together on deck, however, and the schooners were fitted with steel davits from which they could hang.

The cod fishing schooners fought continuously with the Japanese fishing fleet that also worked in the Alaskan waters. The engine noise of the Japanese trawlers scared off the cod and the strings of crab nets — sometimes a mile long — would foul the schooner's anchor lines. The conflict finally erupted in 1938 when the schooner SOPHIE CHRISTENSEN, under the command of Captain J. E. Shields, and the CHARLES R. WILSON with his son, Captain Ed Shields in charge, arrived at the Bering Sea to find the water

covered with Japanese fishing boats and factory ships. Captain Shields Sr. reacted by declaring war on the Japanese, fully three years before the rest of his country. He called by radiotelephone to a cannery in Bristol Bay, Alaska, asking for a telegram to be sent to Seattle:

Bering Sea covered with Japanese fishing boats and nets north of Black Hill. No cutter around. We have God given instincts to shoot straight. Please send dozen high powered rifles. Plenty of ammunition. Duplicate for Wilson.

Captain Shields' message was intercepted by virtually everyone on the coast with a radiotelephone and before long the Seattle newspapers had got hold of the story. The U.S. Coast Guard was very displeased with the situation, and did everything they could to prevent any rifles from being smuggled north to arm Shields' "one man war." The story continued to spread across the country, eventually reaching newspapers in New York.

The international news stories about the Japanese Empire's expansion into China, combined with the furore raised by the media over Captain Shields' declaration of war, inflamed anti-Japanese sentiments among the American public. Before long, the sale of Japanese products in American markets dropped off. The bad publicity was more than the Japanese could stand and they withdrew their fishing fleet from the Bering Sea without a shot being fired. This, of course, was Captain Shields' intent from the beginning.

When the United States entered World War II in December 1941, all of the West Coast fishing schooners, except the CHARLES R. WILSON, were requisitioned by the U.S. government for the war effort. Their masts were removed and they were used as barges. The CHARLES R. WILSON was the only sailing vessel that was engaged in fishing for the duration of the war. Her last voyage was in 1945, after which she was laid up at Poulsbo, Washington. The last of the fishing schooners, the C.A. THAYER, was rebuilt after return-ing at the end of the war. She continued to fish until 1950 when she was laid up beside the CHARLES R. WILSON. The age of fishing under sail was over.

In 1954 the CHARLES R. WILSON was purchased by Mahood, and was towed to the Wolfson Creek log pond. She was beached alongside the CAPILANO where she protected Mahood's log pond for a short period of time. Before long, however, she too was blown down the slope of the beach by the strong southeasters, and like the former Union Steamship, became a hazard to the operation of the booming ground. The CHARLES R. WILSON was broken up where she lay sometime around 1956.

The Motor Minesweepers

Mahood's last attempt to use ships for a breakwater came with the purchase of two former U.S. Navy mine-sweepers. There were 561 of these wood-hulled ves-sels built for use in the Second World War. Because

of their wood construction and small size, they were built at 35 different "yacht yards," rather than larger shipyards. They proved to be a versatile and dura-ble little ship. Used by most of the Allied navies, all of them were built to the same basic design. The main difference between them was in appearance. The first 134 ships built had two stacks, numbers 135 to 445, 480 and 481 had one stack and the remainder had none.

These ships were known as YMS, the designation for a motor minesweeper. The "Y" in the letter group indicates that the ships were service or yard craft. Like the YO and YOG tank barges, the YMS were not given names but were identified by the letter group and their hull number. Later, the vessels that re-mained in service with the U.S. Navy were named. The last of these vessels to be struck from the Navy lists, YMS 327, renamed USS RUFF, served until No-vember 1969.

The YMS were each 136 feet long, had a beam of 24 feet, 6 inches, and a draft of 6 feet, 1 inch. They

One of the YMS Motor Minesweepers at Mahoods booming ground.

Powell River Historical Museum

displaced 320 tons. Two diesel engines, producing 500 horsepower, could drive the ship to 13 knots. The minesweepers carried a complement of four officers and 29 crew.

For armament, a single 3-inch/50-calibre gun and two 20-mm guns were fitted. For defence against submarines, the ships were equipped with two depth charge tracks and two depth charge projectors. Designed for sweeping mines around harbours and inshore in preparation for amphibious assaults, they were also outfitted with an elaborate degaussing system and all the gear needed to cut magnetic and contact mines loose from their anchors.

At the end of the war many of the YMS were sold as surplus vessels and went into civilian service. Some were stripped and converted to barges. Others were converted to yachts by the rich and famous. Still others became workboats, serving as fishing craft, ferries and cargo vessels. Many are still in use, at least two in BC waters, the MV UCHUCK, formerly YMS 123 and the MV MARABELL, a well-known sport-fishing vessel. Perhaps the most famous YMS is the CALYPSO, Jacques Cousteau's first research ship, which is now retired and serves as a part of a maritime museum in France.

The identities of the two YMS that were purchased by Mahood are not known for certain. It is likely that one of them was an unfinished surplus vessel. The other presents a puzzle. Photographs of the ship show the numbers 331 painted on her transom, which would indicate that she is YMS 331.

The Ballard Marine Railway Company of Seattle built the YMS 331, the same yard that built CALYPSO. She was launched on April 24, 1943 and was completed in September of the same year. The minesweeper earned her battle stars during the invasion of Okinawa in April and May 1945. Because so many Destroyers were damaged by the waves of Kamikaze planes that defended the island, their duties were taken over by the larger minesweepers, leaving the smaller YMS to clear the beaches for the invasion. In addition to the Kamikaze, about 400 Shinyo suicide boats were in the area. These speedboats carried one

man and usually a couple of depth charges for explosive. The Shinyo would try to ram the American vessels and detonate their explosives. While they were not very successful, on April 15, YMS 331 was struck and damaged by one of these manned torpedoes. Later, on May 4, an attack by a Kamikaze plane damaged her again. Neither of these attacks caused serious damage to the vessel (serious damage was defined by the Navy as being out of service for more than 30 days).

Official documents tell a contradictory story, however. According to U.S. Maritime Commission and Canadian Customs documents, YMS 331 was sold into British Columbia. A bill of sale shows that she was sold in 1955 to Nelson Brothers Fisheries Limited, of

Was this YMS 331?

Powell River Historical Museum

Vancouver and is apparently still in use as a barge under the name of B.C.P. CARRIER No.17.

Was the ship at Mahood's log pond the YMS 331? Perhaps a deal was struck where the twice-damaged YMS was traded for one in better condition. Mahood was only looking for a breakwater hulk rather than a vessel that would be required to remain afloat as a barge. If the ship at Mahood's log pond was the YMS 331, as the number on her stern would suggest, the official records were never changed. Further research may resolve this matter someday.

Whatever the identities of the ships, in 1955 or '56, two YMS were placed as breakwaters at the Wolfson Creek booming ground. Like the two ships that preceded them it was not long before a couple of good storms had washed them clear across the log pond and up on the beach on the other side. Mahood gave up on the ship breakwater at this point and a rock breakwater was constructed instead. The YMS stayed where they were, about 500 feet apart, until the spring of 1963. The two warships were popular play areas for local children, who couldn't resist climbing aboard to explore. Finally, concerned about the possibility of someone injuring themselves on the ships, Mahood sold them to Roly Meunier for $1 each with the understanding that they would be scrapped.

Meunier stripped all the recoverable metal from the two YMS, saving copper, brass, and lead. Forty-five gallon drums filled with copper nails were sent to the scrap metal dealer. The ships' degaussing system, comprised of copper strips and brass connectors, was salvaged. The ships' tanks were sold for septic tanks. Once all of the metal had been stripped from the hulls, Meunier cut holes in them, stacked driftwood in the holes and set fire to them. When the wooden hulls had been consumed, the beach was raked for globules of lead that had hardened in the sand and any copper or brass pieces that had been missed. For his $1 investment, Meunier recovered $3000 worth of scrap from one of the vessels, somewhat less from the other.

The scrapping of the two YMS hulls has not removed all traces of

Mahood's attempt to use derelict vessels as breakwaters. Partially hidden in the marsh grass at the mouth of Wolfson Creek lies the last vestige of Powell River's "other ship breakwater." The remains of a wooden ship, most likely the old SS CAPILANO II, can still be seen, lying in the silt of the estuary. No longer used as a log pond, the land just east of the former booming ground is now home to a dry land log sort. ⚓

The remains of a wooden ship at the mouth of Wolfson (Lang) Creek.

John A Campbell

Appendix

1   Milestones of the Powell River
        Floating Breakwater

2   American Concrete Ships
        of the First World War Period

3   American Concrete
        Steamships of World War II

4   Concrete Barges of
        World War II

Appendix 1: Milestones in the History of the Powell River Floating Breakwater

1912 Mill begins production. Boomsticks, Davis rafts, scows and barges are moored in front of log pond to provide temporary protection.

1928 Rock breakwater is built.

1930 The hulk of the USS Charleston arrives at Powell River.

1931 USS Huron becomes the second breakwater hulk.

1936 The former log barge Blatchford is anchored south of the government wharf.

1939 Blatchford sinks in the log pond.

1945 Charleston and Huron are moved farther out into the strait, beginning the first reconfiguration of the breakwater. Malahat is brought to Powell River.

1945 Island Carrier is anchored to the north of the Huron.

1946 Malahat is scuttled outside the log pond.

1946 Albertolite is added to the breakwater.

1946 Malaspina joins the breakwater.

1948 The concrete steamships John Smeaton, Henri Le Chatelier, L.J. Vicat and Armand Considere increase the size of the breakwater to nine ships.

1949 Malaspina sinks.

1950 The concrete steamship Thaddeus Merriman joins the fleet.

1951 Malaspina is re-floated – fate unknown.

1954 Island Carrier is exchanged for the hulk of HMCS Coaticook. The former frigate takes Malaspina's place in the breakwater.

1956 The Powell River Company buys the concrete ships P.M. Anderson and Quartz and uses them at the Teakerne Arm booming ground.

1960 Albertolite is removed from the breakwater and cut up for scrap.

1961 Huron sinks in place.

1961 The second major reconfiguration of the breakwater begins. Charleston is moved to Kelsey Bay. Coaticook is removed and scuttled near Victoria.

1961 P.M. Anderson and Quartz are moved from Teakerne Arm to the mill.

1961 YOGN 82 and Peralta join the breakwater.

1961 Cardena takes the Coaticook's place in the breakwater.

1966 The third reconfiguration takes place when the concrete hulks are "bellied" out into the strait. The concrete hulk Emile N. Vidal joins the fleet.

1966 Cardena, the last steel hulk, is moved to Kelsey Bay.

2001 The use of raw logs at the Powell River mill ends.

2002 The breakwater is reconfigured to protect the barge moorage and offloading areas and the foreshore between the rock breakwater and the mill.

Appendix 2: American Concrete Ships of the First World War Period

NAME	BUILDER	CLIENT	DATE	DIMENSIONS (ft)

Faith San Francisco Shipbuilding Co. (Private) March 1918 320 x 44.5 x 27.7
The first American concrete ship. Operated around the world until 1921. Stripped and towed to Cuba for use as a breakwater.

Atlantus Liberty Shipbuilding Co. (USSB) April 1918 249.3 x 43.5 x 22.5
Operated in the coal trade 1920-21. Laid up and stripped in 1925. Towed to Cape May, New Jersey in 1926 for use as breakwater. Her wreck is a popular tourist attraction there today.

Polias Fougner Concrete Shipbldg Co. (USSB) May 1919 267.3 x 46 x 23.4
Operated in the coal trade early 1920. On her fifth trip she went off course and went aground on Old Cilley Ledge, Port Clyde, Maine. Was stuck on ledge for a few years, then rolled off into deep water.

Palo Alto San Francisco Shipbuilding Co. (USSB) May 1919 420 x 54 x 35
Laid up at San Francisco until 1924 when she was sold for scrapping. Towed to Aptos, California, 1930, grounded and connected to shore with a long pier and fitted with dance floor, arcade, swimming pool and dining room. Used since 1932 as a fishing pier. Remains a popular tourist attraction in Monterey Bay.

Selma Fred T. Ley & Co. (USSB) June 1919 420.7 x 54 x 34.4
Tore sixty feet of her bottom out on a jetty at Tampico, 1920. Temporarily repaired and towed to Galveston. Grounded on the Pelican Flats where she remains today. Designated a State Archaeological Landmark in 1992.

Latham Fred T. Ley & Co. (USSB) June 1919 420.7 x 54 x 34.4
Struck the same jetty at Tampico as Selma, 1920, punching holes in her bottom. Steamed to Galveston under her own power for repairs. Ended up in New Orleans used as floating oil storage tank in 1924. Location today is unknown.

Cape Fear Liberty Shipbuilding Co. (USSB) July 1919 266.6 x 46 x 24.8
Operated in the coal trade on the east coast. Collided with steamship, City of Atlanta in Narragansett Bay and sank in 125 fathoms of water.

Old North State/Sapona Liberty Shipbuilding Co. (USSB) Oct 1919 266.6 x 46 x 24.8
Operated briefly in the coal trade. Sold for use as oil storage hull in Miami, Florida, 1924, but was towed to the Bahamas for use as liquor warehouse. Was grounded in a hurricane, 1926. Used as a bombing target during WW2. Popular fishing and diving site today.

Cuyamaca Pacific Marine Construction Co. (USSB) June 1920 420.7 x 54 x 34.3
Operated in the Gulf of Mexico oil trade 1920-21. Laid up and dismantled 1924 and used as floating oil tank at New Orleans. Listed as scrapped in 1926. Location today is unknown.

NAME	BUILDER	CLIENT	DATE	DIMENSIONS (ft)
San Pasqual	Pacific Marine Construction Co.	(USSB)	June 1920	420.7 x 54 x 34.3

Operated in the Gulf of Mexico oil trade 1920-21. Damaged in a storm and laid up until 1924, sold for use as molasses store ship in Cuba. Dismantled and used as depot ship at Havana in 1932 and then was grounded in 1933. Fitted with machine guns and cannons during WW2 and used as a lookout for German Subs, connected to shore by a bridge. Used as a prison ship during the Cuban revolution. Used as a sportsman's club and site for fishing competitions after the revolution. Converted to an offshore hotel in the 1990s and still in use.

Dinsmore	A. Bently & Sons Co.	(USSB)	June 1920	420 x 54 x 35

Used as an oil storage terminal at Mobile until 1932. Stripped and used as a breakwater in Texas.

Moffitt	A. Bently & Sons Co.	(USSB)	July 1920	420 x 54 x 35

Moved to the Gulf of Mexico, 1921. Laid up until 1924. Stripped and used as an oil barge at New Orleans. Location today unknown.

Durham	MacDonald Engineering Works	(Private)	July 1920	290.2 x 33.9 x 22

Found to be so under-powered that she was converted to a barge. Scrapped and abandoned a few years later.

Peralta	San Francisco Shipbldg Co.	(USSB)	Oct 1920	420 x 54 x 35

See Chapter Seven.

Darlington	MacDonald Engin. Works	(Private)	Nov 1920	290.2 x 33.9 x 22

Never completed. Abandoned near Aransas Pass, 1922.

USQMC	Newport Shipbuilding Co.	(Private)	1921	300.1 x 44 x 24
Tanker No.1/McKittrick				

Operated briefly in the oil trade. Dismantled and operated as an offshore nightclub in 1932. Wrecked in a storm on Point Romain.

Appendix 3:   American Concrete Steamships of World War II

Builder: *McCloskey & Company, Tampa, Florida*

NAME	LAUNCHED	DESCRIPTION
Vitruvius	July 1943	Made 2 trips between Cuba and the US carrying sugar. Sunk as a blockship at Normandy during the Allied invasion.
David O. Saylor	July 1943	Not used in active service. Sunk as a blockship at Normandy during the Allied invasion.
Arthur Newell Talbot	July 1943	Opcrated in the sugar trade for 3 months. Sent to the west coast for use as a training ship for the Army. Laid up at Mobile after the war until 1948, when she was sunk as a breakwater at Kiptopeke, VA.
Richard Lewis Humphrey	Sept 1943	Carried sugar and coffee before being sent to the west coast for use as a training ship by the Army. Was slightly damaged in a hurricane and was laid up at San Francisco in June 1945. Sold to the Mexican government in 1950 and presumed to have been scrapped and broken up.
Richard Kidder Meade	Sept 1943	Operated in the sugar trade briefly before being used as an Army training ship on the west coast. Laid up at Mobile after the war and sunk as a breakwater at Kiptopeke, VA in 1949.
Willis A. Slater	Sept 1943	Operated as a sulphur carrier before being assigned to a convoy to England. Was involved in a collision with Vitruvius and put into Bermuda for repairs. Sent to the west coast for use as an Army training ship. Sunk as a breakwater at Kiptopeke, VA in 1949.
Leonard Chase Wason	Nov 1943	Operated in the Gulf of Mexico and later assigned to the US Army for the duration of the war. Laid up after the war's end and sold in 1948. Sunk as a breakwater at Kiptopeke, VA in 1949.
John Smeaton	Nov 1943	See Chapter Seven.
Joseph Aspdin	Nov 1943	Operated in the merchant trade, during which she sailed through a hurricane, in winds to 120 mph with minimal damage. Was later assigned to the US Army for use as a storeship in the South Pacific. After the war, was laid up at Astoria, Oregon. Broke free of her moorings at Yaquina Bay and was stranded and sunk on North Reef. She was a total loss.
John Grant	Jan 1944	Operated in the merchant trade until being assigned to the US Army. Laid up at Tampa until 1949, when she was sunk as a breakwater at Kiptopeke, VA.
Henri Le Chatelier	Jan 1944	See Chapter Seven.

NAME	LAUNCHED	DESCRIPTION
L.J. Vicat	Jan 1944	See Chapter Seven.
Robert Whitman Lesley	March 1944	Operated briefly in the merchant trade and then converted for use as an Army storeship. Served in the South Pacific. Laid up after the war until being sunk as a breakwater at Kiptopeke, VA in 1949.
Edwin Thacher	March 1944	Operated in the merchant trade before being assigned to the US Army for use as a storeship. Laid up after the war until being sunk as a breakwater at Kiptopeke, VA in 1949.
C.W. Pasley	March 1944	Converted for use as an Army storeship and operated in the South Pacific. Laid up at Seattle after the war until being sunk as a pier at Yaquina Bay, Newport, Oregon in 1948.
Armand Considere	May 1944	See Chapter Seven.
Francois Hennebique	May 1944	Delivered directly to the US Army with no private operator. Used as a storeship in the South Pacific during the war and voyaged to Japan post war. Laid up at San Francisco until 1948 when she was sunk as a dock at Yaquina Bay, Newport, Oregon. The Yaquina Bay Dock and Dredge Co used her superstructure as office space.
P.M. Anderson	May 1944	See Chapter Seven.
Albert Kahn	July 1944	Used by the US Army in the South Pacific as a storeship. Voyaged to Japan post war. She was severely damaged in a typhoon at Saipan in Sept. 1946 and was scuttled in deep water by the Army in March 1947.
Willard A. Pollard	July 1944	Used by the US Army in the South Pacific as a storeship. Laid up after the war until 1948. Sunk as a breakwater at Kiptopeke, VA in 1949.
William Foster Cowham	July 1944	Used by the US Army in the South Pacific as a storeship. Laid up after the war until 1948. Sunk as a breakwater at Kiptopeke, VA in 1949.
Edwin Clarence Eckel	Sept 1944	Used by the US Army in the South Pacific as a storeship. In November 1946 while en route from Shanghai to San Francisco carrying a cargo of ammunition and explosives, she was reported disabled with rudder damage. Was towed to Yokohama where she was declared a total loss. She was stripped and scuttled in deep water in January 1947.
Thaddeus Merriman & Emile N. Vidal	Sept 1944	See Chapter Seven.

Appendix 4:   US Maritime Commission Concrete Barges of World War II

Type B7-D1   Builder: *Barrett & Hilp, Belair Shipyard (San Francisco, CA)*

YARD	SERVICE	NAME	DESCRIPTION
1	Aug 1943	**Agate**	Operated as floating warehouse by US Army in the South Pacific.
2	Sept 1943	**Chromite**	Operated as floating warehouse by US Army in the South Pacific.
3	Sept 1943	**Flint**	Assigned to US Navy Bureau of Docks Construction Equipment.
4	Sept 1943	**Granite**	Operated as floating warehouse by US Army in the South Pacific.
5	Oct 1943	**Graphite**	Assigned to US Navy Bureau of Docks Construction Equipment.
6	Oct 1943	**Gypsum**	Assigned to US Navy Bureau of Docks Construction Equipment.
7	Nov 1943	**Mica**	Operated as floating warehouse by US Army in the South Pacific.
8	June 1944	**Bauxite (II) IX154**	Used by the Navy as a floating warehouse in the South Pacific.
9	June 1944	**Asphalt IX153**	Used by the Navy as a floating warehouse in the South Pacific. Sunk in a typhoon at Saipan Oct. 1944.
10	May 1944	Slate, renamed **Carmita IX152**	Used by the Navy as a floating warehouse in the South Pacific. Lost at sea March 1947.
11	March 1944	Midnight (III), renamed **Trefoil IX 149**	Used by the Navy as a floating warehouse in the South Pacific. Used to house workers building dry-docks at Apra Harbour in 1946. Sold to the Asia Development Co., Shanghai in 1948.
12	April 1944	**Quartz IX150**	See Chapter Nine.
13	June 1944	Bauxite (I), renamed **Silica IX 151**	Used by the Navy as a floating warehouse in the South Pacific specialising in medical supplies. Was driven aground at Buckner Bay, Okinawa by a typhoon in Oct. 1945. Damaged beyond repair. Towed to sea and scuttled.
14	July 1944	Limestone (I), renamed **Corundum IX 164**	Used by the Navy as a floating warehouse in the South Pacific. Used to store landing craft and vehicle spare parts.
15	Aug 1944	**Feldspar IX159**	Used by the Navy as a floating warehouse in the South Pacific. Specialised in Army and Marine corps supplies.
16	Aug 1944	**Marl IX160**	Used by the Navy as a floating warehouse in the South Pacific. Caught in a typhoon while under tow from Leyte to Okinawa in Sept. 1945. Broke away from her tow. Later salvaged and towed to Subic Bay and laid up. Sold to Asia Development Co., Philippines in 1948.
17	Aug 1944	**Barite IX161**	Used by the Navy as a floating warehouse in the South Pacific.
18	Sept 1944	**Lignite IX162**	Used by the Navy as a floating warehouse in the South Pacific. Grounded by a typhoon at Buckner Bay, Okinawa in Oct. 1945. Refloated and towed to Hong Kong and then to Luzon in 1946.
19	Sept 1944	**Cinnabar IX163**	Used by the Navy as a floating warehouse in the South Pacific. Grounded by a typhoon at Baten Ko, Okinawa in Oct. 1945.
20	Oct 1944	**Limestone (II) IX158**	Used by the Navy as a floating warehouse in the South Pacific and at Bikini Atoll.

Builder: *Concrete Ship Constructors Inc. (National City, California)*

Type B7-A2

All were operated by the US Navy as tanker barges.

YARD	NAME
1	Concrete No. 1
2	Concrete No. 2, renamed YO 144
3	Concrete No. 3, renamed YOG 40
4	Concrete No. 4, renamed YOG 41
5	Concrete No. 5, renamed YOG 42
6	YOG 145
7	YOG 146
8	YOG 53
9	YO 159
10	YO 160
11	YO 161
12	YO 162
13	YO 163
14	YO 182
15	YO 183
16	YOG 82
17	YO 184
18	YO 185
19	YOG 83
20	YO 186
21	YO 187
22	YOG 84

Type B5-BJ1

All operated by the US Army as floating warehouses and supply lighters.

YARD	NAME
23	Carbon BCL3049
24	Barium BCL 3050
25	Helium BCL 3051
26	Nitrogen BCL 3052
27	Radium BCL 3053
28	Argon BCL 3054
29	Cadmium BCL 3055
30	Chromium BCL 3056
31	Cobalt BCL 3057
32	Iridium BCL 3058
33	Lithium BCL 3059
34	Magnesium BCL 3060
35	Neon BCL 3061
36	Nickel BCL 3062
37	Phosphorus BCL 3063
38	Sodium BCL 3064
39	Sulphur BCL 3065
40	Tellurium BCL 3066
41	Tungsten BCL 3067
42	Uranium BCL 3068
43	Bismuth BCL 3069
44	Bromide BCL 3070

Type B5-BJ2

Operated by the US Army as refrigerated floating warehouses.

YARD	NAME
45	Hydrogen BCL 3071
46	Calcium BCL 3072
47	Antimony BCL 3073

Type B5-BJ3

Operated by the US Army as maintenance lighters.

YARD	NAME
48	Cerium FMS 1
49	Radon FMS 2

Builder: *MacEvoy Shipbuilding Corp. (Savannah, Georgia)*

Type B7-A1

Operated by the US Navy as Tanker Barges. Concretes No. 7 to No. 12 assigned to the Bureau of Docks Construction Equipment.

YARD	NAME	YARD	NAME
1	Concrete No. 6	5	Concrete No. 10
2	Concrete No. 7	6	Concrete No. 11
3	Concrete No. 8	7	Concrete No. 12
4	Concrete No. 9		

Builder: *McCloskey & Company (Houston, Texas)*

Type B7-A1

Operated by the US Navy as Tanker Barges — Assigned to the Bureau of Docks Construction Equipment

YARD	NAME	YARD	NAME
1	Concrete No. 29	3	Concrete No. 31
2	Concrete No. 30	4	Concrete No. 32

Glossary

Aggregate Any of several hard inert materials (as sand, gravel, or slag) used for mixing with a cementing material to form concrete, mortar, or plaster.

ASDIC An underwater echo sounding device developed during the First World War and named for the Anti-Submarine Detection Investigation Committee, the group of British, French, and American scientists who developed it. The name has been universally replaced by the American term SONAR. (See SONAR)

Ballast A heavy substance used to improve the stability and control the draft of a ship.

Bamfield Cable Station In 1902 the longest undersea communications cable in the world was laid between the Bamfield Cable Station at Bamfield, British Columbia, and Fanning Island, 4000 miles away. From Fanning Island, the cable continued on to Fiji, New Zealand, and Australia. During the First World War the German Cruiser NUREMBERG landed a raiding party at the Fanning Island end of the cable, blowing up the power station and cutting the cable, towing the ends out to sea. There was great concern after this that a similar raid could take place at Bamfield and the cable station became a heavily guarded part of the coast during the war.

Barge A roomy, often flat-bottomed vessel used chiefly for the transport of goods and usually propelled by a towing vessel. The word can also be used to describe a motorboat supplied to the flag officer of a flagship.

Beam The width of a boat or ship at its widest part.

Boom A large raft of logs built to allow storage or transport of the logs. They are built to several different patterns, depending on the boom's purpose. A boom can be as simple as a "bag" formed by boom sticks where logs can be stored before being fed to the mill or placed into larger booms for towing. Flat booms held together with cables and boom sticks can be used to move logs short distances in favourable weather. Davis rafts and bundle booms are used for longer distances where bad weather might be encountered.

Booming grounds A protected log pond where logs are sorted and placed into booms for transport to mills for processing.

Boom stick A long straight log with holes bored through each end to allow it to be connected to other boom sticks using a boom chain. The connected boom sticks are used to contain loose logs for storage or sorting and can be used when building a boom for transport.

Bosun, Bo'sun, Boatswain The officer aboard a ship who is responsible for the maintenance of the vessel and its fittings. The word originated in the 17th Century when ships were required by law to carry three boats, named respectively the boat, the cock, and the skiff. The men in charge of them were the Boatswain, Cockswain, and Skiffswain, swain meaning lover or keeper.

Bridge A raised transverse platform from which a boat or ship is navigated. A vessel's bridge can be open or enclosed by a cabin.

Bulkhead An upright partition or wall that separates compartments. Watertight bulkheads on a ship prevent water from filling the whole hull in the event of serious damage.

Calibre The diameter of a bullet or other projectile, or the diameter of the bore of a gun. Calibre is expressed in inches or millimetres. In the case of artillery, the length of a gun's barrel may be expressed as calibre, for example a 6-inch/50 calibre gun is a gun with a six inch bore (calibre) and a barrel that is 50 calibres (300 inches) in length.

Cargo, bulk Cargo such as grain, ore, or coal that is placed in the ship's holds with no other containment or packaging.

Cargo, general any cargo on a ship other than bulk cargo.

CGS The acronym for Canadian Government Ship, used to identify vessels under the command of the Canadian government. After the formation of the Royal Canadian Coast Guard, the acronym CCGS, for Canadian Coast Guard Ship, came into use.

Chips Small pieces of wood used for the production of pulp for papermaking.

Commission To place a ship into active service.

ComSerRon A US Naval abbreviation for Commander Service Squadron.

Concrete A construction material formed of a mix of aggregate materials bonded with cement.

Concrete, reinforced Normally refers to a type of construction where steel reinforcing bars are placed inside forms, which are then filled with concrete. Concrete is very strong in compression but needs the steel reinforcing to give it the tensile strength to prevent cracking.

Cruiser A type of warship, originally attached to a fleet to provide reconnaissance. Cruisers were typically fast, strongly armed vessels and were built in several categories. The largest were the Armoured Cruisers which were in fact battleships. They were heavily armoured and in later years the class was renamed Battle Cruisers. The Protected Cruisers were smaller and less heavily armoured, except at the waterline. Smallest were the Light Cruisers with little armour plating, but very fast. As aerial reconnaissance has replaced the Cruisers' original function with the fleet, the class has become a small battleship, equipped with guided missiles as armament.

Cruising radius The distance that a ship can travel at cruising speed fully loaded and starting with full fuel tanks. Cruising radius is measured in days.

Davis Raft A type of log boom designed by BC logger G.G. Davis. The Davis Raft was capable of withstanding much heavier weather than flat booms and so was used extensively to transport logs from the Queen Charlotte Islands to the mills of southern BC. A Davis Raft consisted of a mat of logs woven together with steel cables. Logs were piled on top in layers and the whole raft was then securely wrapped. The rafts could reach lengths of more than 130 feet.

DEMS An acronym for Defensively Equipped Merchant Ship. During World War II, Canadian and British merchant vessels were equipped with guns for defence which were manned by naval volunteers known as DEMS gunners. The gunners were assisted by the crewmembers of the ship.

Dory A type of rowed boat used extensively in the North American East Coast fisheries. A dory is easily identified by its flat, lengthways-planked bottom and its flared sides. Dories usually have removable thwarts, allowing them to be nested together on the deck of a schooner to save space.

Dry land sort An area where logs can be sorted and stored before transport to the sawmill, the land based equivalent of a booming ground.

Dumb A term used when referring to an unpowered vessel.

Ferro-cement, Ferro-concrete Normally refers to a type of construction utilising a steel framework of reinforcing bar, covered with a wire mesh. Mortar is applied to the mesh by trowelling, forming the hull of the vessel.

Forecastle, fo'c'sle The forward part of a ship, often where the crew is housed. The name originates from the days when actual raised castles were built at the forward and after ends of warships where men could throw spears and rocks and shoot arrows down onto the decks of an enemy ship.

Fuller's earth Aluminum Magnesium Silicate, a naturally mined clay often used as a filtering and refining agent for animal, vegetable, and mineral oils. Also used as an absorbent medium. So named because of its early use as a fulling agent when making cloth.

Graving dock A basin, connected to the water through large doors into which a ship may be floated. Once in the graving dock, the water can be pumped out and the ship supported on blocking, allowing maintenance and repairs to be made.

Hawse pipe The fitting at the bow of a ship through which passes its anchor chains and cables.

Hog fuel Waste wood from a sawmill, which is used as a fuel for boilers. Hog fuel was named for the machines used to make it, known as hogs because of the way that they would "eat" whatever was thrown into them and the grunting noise produced as wood went through them. The use of hog fuel as a primary boiler fuel was pioneered at the Powell River mill in the early 1920s and the mill became the first to import the fuel from sawmills around the coast.

HMCS The acronym for His/Her Majesty's Canadian Ship, which identifies a vessel as a Canadian Naval ship.

Keelson A longitudinal support structure in a vessel, running above and fastened to the keel, which serves to stiffen and strengthen the framework.

Knot One nautical mile or one nautical mile per hour.

Liberty Ship A type of steel merchant ship that was built during the Second World War to a British design that dated back to 1879. Liberty ships could be built quickly and from prefabricated parts, allowing the speedy replacement of ships that were lost to enemy action. They were 441.5 feet in length, had a beam of 57 feet, and were capable of a speed of 11 knots. There were 2770 Liberty ships built during the war.

Lighter A "dumb" or unpowered vessel used to transfer freight from ship to shore or vice versa.

Log Crib An enclosure built of timber and used for the storage and transport of smaller wood, such as pulp blocks or shingle bolts.

Log dump A place where logs can be dumped into the water so that they can be put into booms.

Log haul A conveyor used to pull logs out of the log pond and into the mill. Also known as jackladders and log conveyors, they are made of a continuous loop of chain, fitted with serrated flights to grip the logs. Usually powered by electric motors, in earlier times they were run by reciprocating steam engines.

Log pond sludge In the days before environmental standards and controls, industrial plants discharged the waste materials from their operation directly to the environment. At Powell River, this meant that all the mill's sewers flowed directly to the ocean in front of the mill. The calm water created by the breakwater created a perfect settling pond for this material, which consisted of wood pulp dumped from tanks, ash from the boilers, chemicals from the pulping process and waste wood. It was estimated in the 1940s that fully five per cent of the mill's total effluent ended up settling in the log pond. This made regular and frequent dredging necessary as the sludge gradually filled the log pond in.

Naval Armed Guard On American merchant ships during the Second World War, guns were manned by members of the Naval Armed Guard. Unlike the DEMS gunners of the Canadian and British merchant ships, the Naval armed Guard were not assisted by the crew of the ship.

Outfitting After a ship is launched, it is moved to the outfitting dock where work on the vessel such as installation of equipment, finishing of cabins, and set-up of control devices is completed. Once the ship has been outfitted, it is ready to undergo its sea trials.

Pile driver A piece of machinery used to drive pilings into the ground or seabed by striking with a weight.

Poop Deck The after deck of a ship. On sailing ships, the poop deck was where the helmsman stood to steer the ship. A large wave coming over the stern would occasionally carry away a ship's wheel and helmsman and gave rise to the term "pooped" to describe how one felt when so tired that he could barely function. The poop deck got its name from the Roman practice of carrying small images of their gods, known as pupi, there for luck.

Pre-Dreadnought Era The launching of the British Battleship, HMS Dreadnought on October 1, 1906 instantly rendered all other battleships obsolete. The Dreadnought was the first warship to be powered exclusively by steam turbine engines, giving her an advantage in speed. She was also the most heavily armed ship to that time, carrying ten 12-inch guns, giving her accurate fire at great distances. The Dreadnought was so revolutionary that all ships of similar design are referred to as dreadnoughts. Vessels of the Pre-Dreadnought Era were fitted with a few large guns, and many smaller calibre guns for delivering broadside attacks at close range.

Ripple Rock A twin-peaked rock that extended into Seymour Narrows near Campbell River, BC and created what Captain George Vancouver called in the late 1700s, "one of the vilest stretches of water in the world." Tidal currents flowing past the rock formed whirlpools and eddies that resulted in the loss of 120 vessels and 114 lives between 1875 and 1958. Finally, between November 1955 and April 1958, a tunnel was dug from nearby Maud Island, under Seymour Narrows, and up under Ripple Rock. The peaks of the rock were packed with 1375 tons of explosives. On April 5, 1958, the largest non-nuclear explosion in history was set off and Ripple Rock ceased to exist.

Sardines, California The California sardine industry was devastated in 1944/45 when the remaining stocks of sardines declined rapidly. Over-fishing had resulted in as many as 75 per cent of adult fish being caught and a failure of the remaining fish to spawn resulted in the destruction of the fishery by the 1950s.

Schooner A type of sailing vessel, typically with two or more masts, all rigged with fore and aft sails. A two-masted schooner will have a foremast that is shorter than the mainmast. Schooners were built with as many as seven masts, but these were found to be very unwieldy.

Scuttle To dispose of a vessel by deliberately sinking it. The word has its origins in the old Anglo-Saxon word meaning, "hole."

Sea trials Once a vessel has been outfitted it goes out on its sea trials where its performance and handling are judged in relation to its design specifications. Once sea trials are complete, it is ready to be commissioned.

Shanghai To be pressed into service against one's will. The word originated in the Chinese port of Shanghai. American clipper captains who couldn't find enough sailors to leave port would pay the owners of bars to slip drugs into the drinks of drunken sailors. The unconscious men would be put aboard the ship, and awaken to find themselves at sea.

SONAR An underwater echo sounding device. Its name is an acronym for SOnic Navigation And Ranging.

Spall To break up into chips or fragments.

SS Acronym identifying a vessel as a steamship.

Tanker Ship designed for transport of liquid cargoes.

Teredo Also known as a shipworm, the teredo is actually a species of bivalve. It burrows into and eats wood that is submerged, quickly rendering logs useless for anything other than hog fuel. Teredos die soon after being removed from the water. An odour that no one who has worked in a west-coast sawmill will forget is the stench of a "teredo log" that has just gone through the mill.

Three island ship A term used to describe a ship with a raised poop, bridge, and forecastle, so called because when the hull of the ship was obscured by swells or the horizon, it appeared as a group of three islands.

Tons, dead weight The amount of cargo, fuel, water, stores, crew, etc. that a vessel can carry when fully loaded. Dead weight tonnage is expressed in tons of 2240 pounds.

Tons, displacement The weight of the volume of water that is displaced by a ship as it floats. A ton is equal to 35 cubic feet of seawater or 35.9 cubic feet of fresh water. Displacement tons are always 2240 pounds.

Tons, gross The total internal capacity of a ship expressed in "tons" of 100 cubic feet is its gross registered tonnage. Originally this term had nothing to do with weight or the displacement of a vessel but indicated the size of a ship by the number of tuns (barrels) that could be stowed aboard.

Townsite Housing built and owned by a company to house workers and their families. While some companies built townsites with small, cheaply constructed dwellings, the Powell River Company built their townsite following the "Green City" concept and incorporated green spaces, commercial buildings, recreational facilities and well constructed, attractive houses with the intention of attracting workers to come to Powell River and stay. The company sold the houses in the Townsite in 1955. While the companies that owned them razed most other industrial townsites, private ownership at Powell River has allowed the Townsite to survive as one of the last intact examples of an early 20th century industrial town, with about 400 residential and commercial buildings. The Townsite was designated as a National Historic District in 1995, the only community in Western Canada to receive this honour.

Triple expansion engine A reciprocating steam engine in which the steam is expanded in three stages to produce power. A triple expansion engine will have high-pressure, intermediate-pressure and low-pressure cylinders and exhausts into a condenser at less than atmospheric pressure.

Undocumented Unregistered.

USAT The acronym for United States Army Transport, used to identify vessels of the American Army Transport Service.

US Maritime Administration The organisation that succeeded the US Maritime Commission in 1950 and is still in operation today.

US Maritime Commission The organisation that succeeded the United States Shipping Board in 1936.

USMSTS The acronym for United States Maritime Service Training School.

USS The acronym for United States Ship, used to identify an American naval vessel.

US Shipping Board The organisation formed during World War I to control and direct the operation and expansion of American shipping.

Victory Ship Later in the Second World War, a less spartan and faster design of merchant vessel was being built as well as the Liberty ships. The Victory ships were 455 feet long, 62 feet wide, and could reach speeds of 16 knots powered by a steam turbine. There were 534 Victory ships built between early 1944 and the end of the war.

War Shipping Administration The organisation formed during World War II to direct all American wartime merchant shipping.

Sources

1. A Breakwater of Ships

Bradley, Ken, and Karen Southern, *Powell River's Railway Era.* Victoria, BC, The BC
   Railway Historical Association, 2000.

NorskeCanada, *The Millennium Project* files.

The Powell River Historical Museum, *Records of the Powell River Company.*

2. The U.S. Cruisers

"A Battleship for a Breakwater," *The Powell River Digester,* November 1930.

Brewer, Charles B. "Six Hundred Tons of Barnacles," *Harper's Weekly,* 24 October 1910.

Clapp, Frank A., *Research Files,* Victoria, BC

Defieux, Charles M. "Of Men and Ships; No One Can Get Emotional About Ships of
   Cement," *The Vancouver Sun,* 19 June 1965.

The Dictionary of American Naval Fighting Ships, Volume II. U.S. Naval Historical Center,
   1959-1991.

Hartwell, Joe. *Remembering the sounds of my grandfather's footsteps,* [Online]
   freepages.military.rootsweb.com/~caunithistories/index.htm.

Jane's Fighting Ships 1928, London: Jane's Publications.

Moore, John, ed. *Jane's Fighting Ships of World War One,* London: Jane's Publications, 1990.

NorskeCanada.

Olson, Oren. Interview by John A. Campbell.

The Powell River Historical Museum.

3. The First World War Wooden Freighter

Clapp, Frank A. "British Columbia's Early Log Barges, Part 1," *The Sea Chest,* Journal
   of the Puget Sound Maritime Historical Society, March 2001.

Clapp, Frank A. "British Columbia's Early Log Barges, Part 2," *The Sea Chest,* Journal
   of the Puget Sound Maritime Historical Society, June 2001.

Hurley, Edward N. *The Bridge to France,* Philadelphia & London: J.B. Lippencott
   Company, 1927.

NorskeCanada.

4. The Windjammers

Clapp, Frank A. "Log Barges, Parts 1 & 2."

Clapp. Research Files.

"The Genesis of the Wooden Shipbuilding Industry in British Columbia." *The
   Timberman,* September 1917.

Gibson, Gordon and Carol Renison. *Bull of the Woods.* Douglas and McIntyre, 1980.

Greene, Ruth. *Personality Ships of British Columbia.* West Vancouver: Marine Tapestry Publications Limited, 1969.

Henry, Tom. *Westcoasters: Boats That Built BC.* Madeira Park, BC: Harbour Publishing, 1998.

Huycke Jr., Harold D. To Santa Rosalia, *Further and Back.* Newport News, Virginia: The Mariner's Museum, 1970.

Lowther, Bruce. "The Ship That Had a Garden." *The Victoria Colonist,* 28 November 1954.

McDonald, Captain Daniel J. "A Million Miles Under Sail." *Sea Breezes, The Magazine of Ships and the Sea,* Volume 47, 1973.

NorskeCanada.

Olson. Interview.

The Powell River Historical Museum.

Thompson, Bill. *Once Upon a Stump, Times and Tales of Powell River Pioneers,* Powell River Heritage Research Association, 1993.

The Vancouver Maritime Museum Collection.

5. The Steel Ships

Appleton, Thomas E. *Usque Ad Mare: A History of the Canadian Coast Guard and Marine Services.* The Department of Transport, 1968.

"Capitol Iron: Scrap Dealers in Lotusland." *Resolution, The Newsletter of the Maritime Museum of British Columbia,* #18 February 1990.

Clapp. Research Files.

Dunn, Arthur. "Memories of the Old Malaspina." *Powell River's First 50 Years.* Powell River, The Powell River News Limited, 1960.

Ferguson, Ian. Ian Ferguson's Homepage, Part 1, SS Albertolite, [Online] members.tripod.com/~merchantships2/ian/ianfergusonshomepage1.html.

Jane's Fighting Ships 1925, London: Jane's Publications.

Jane's Fighting Ships 1939, London: Jane's Publications.

Lloyd's Register of Shipping — 1913/14, 1914/15, 1918/19, 1929/30, 1933/34.

MacPherson, Ken. *Frigates of the Royal Canadian Navy, 1943 – 1974.* St. Catherines, Ontario: Vanwell Publishing Co.

Montieth, Bob. Interview by John A. Campbell.

NorskeCanada.

Olson. Interview.

Patterson, T.W. "If Derelicts Could Speak." *The Victoria Daily Colonist,* 19 March 1972.

The Powell River Historical Museum.

Rees, S. "At Sea With B.C.'s Fishery Patrol." *The Powell River Digester,* September and October 1929.

Twigg, Arthur M. *Union Steamships Remembered: 1920 –1958.* Artery Enterprises, 1997.

6. American Concrete Shipbuilding

Anderson, Arthur R. *Prestressed Concrete Floating Structures (State of the Art),* The Society of Naval Architects and Marine Engineers, 1975.

Assessment of Concrete Hulks. Metro Testing Laboratories Ltd., Burnaby, BC, 31 October 2002.

Concrete Afloat. London: Thomas Telford Limited, 1977.

Haviland, Jean. "American Concrete Steamers of the First and Second World Wars." *American Neptune Magazine,* #22, 1962.

Hurley, *The Bridge to France.*

Sawyer, L.A. and W.H. Mitchell. *From America to United States: The History of the Long-Range Merchant Shipbuilding Program of the United States Maritime Commission (1937 – 1952)* Part 2, London: The World Ship Society, 1981.

Turner, Colin W.R. "American Concrete Tankers." *Sea Breezes, The Magazine of Ships and the Sea,* December 1996, January 1997.

Tuthill, Lewis H. "Concrete Operations in the Concrete Ship Program." *Journal of the American Concrete Institute,* January 1945.

Williams, William J. "The American Concrete Shipbuilding Program of World War I." *American Neptune Magazine,* #52, 1992.

7. The Concrete Steamships of World War II

Assessment of Concrete Hulks.

Bozard, Andrew. Correspondence with John A. Campbell.

Concrete Afloat.

Dolmage, Captain Bill. "Letter from Captain Bill Dolmage." *Westcoast Mariner,* January 1991.

Grover, David H. *U.S. Army Ships and Watercraft of World War II.* Annapolis, Maryland: The Naval Institute Press, 1987.

Hacking, Norman. "Peaceful Purpose for Wartime Fleet." *The Vancouver Province,* 5 November 1975.

Haviland. "American Concrete Steamers."

McKaig, James B. "Biography of James B. McKaig." [Online] www.armed-guard.com/biogm.html.

Montieth. Interview.

Moore, Jim. Correspondence with John A. Campbell.

NorskeCanada.

Owens, Gene. "Concrete Hulled Vessels Have Made Their Mark on Maritime History." *The Mobile Register,* 2 June 2002.

The Powell River Historical Museum.

Powers, Richard R. D-Day 1944 and Why They Owe Me a Trip on the Queen Mary. [Online] www.usmm.org/concrete.html.

Rau, William N. "Blockships at Normandy." *Steamboat Bill Magazine,* 1994.

Sawyer and Mitchell. *From America to United States.*

Tuthill. "Concrete Operations."

"12-Year-Old Ship Breakwater Bound, Reluctant to End." *Marine Digest,* 11 August 1956.

The U.S. Maritime Administration. *U.S. Maritime Commission files* #901-11883, 901-15775, 901-7421 and 901- 11823.

"U.S. Researcher Discovers Powell River Breakwater Fleet Treasure Trove." *MacMillan Bloedel News,* January 1973.

Wynne, Lewis N. and Carolyn J. Baimes. "Regional Sea Stories, Still They Sail: Shipbuilding in Tampa During World War II, A Story of Gulf Coast Maritime History." *The Gulf Coast Historical Review,* Spring 1990.

8. The Concrete Tanker of World War I

Assessment of Concrete Hulks.

Dolmage. "Letter."

Haviland. "American Concrete Steamers."

Heron, David W. *Forever Facing South – The Story of the SS Palo Alto "The Old Cement Ship of Seacliff Beach."* Otter B Books, 1991.

Hurley. *The Bridge to France.*

Montieth. Interview.

NorskeCanada.

9. The Concrete Barges

Carter, Worral Reed, Rear Admiral. *Beans, Bullets, and Black Oil: The Story of Fleet Logistics Afloat in the Pacific During World War II.* Washington DC, Department of the Navy, 1953.

Department of the Navy, Naval Historical Center. [Online] www.history.navy.mil/faqs/faq82-2.htm.

The Dictionary of American Naval Fighting Ships, Volume V. U.S. Naval Historical Center, 1959-1991.

Grover. *U.S. Army Ships.*

NorskeCanada.

Partin, John R. Correspondence with John A. Campbell.

Sawyer and Mitchell. *From America to United States.*

Tuthill. "Concrete Operations."

The United States Maritime Administration. *U.S. Maritime Commission file #901-14233.*

United States Department of the Interior National Park Service. *The Archeology of the Atomic Bomb, A Submerged Cultural Resources Assessment of the Sunken Fleet of Operation Crossroads at Bikini and Kwajalein Atoll Lagoons,* By James P. Delgado, Daniel J. Lenihan and Larry E. Murphy. U.S. National Park Service Submerged Cultural Resources Unit, National Maritime Initiative, Santa Fe, New Mexico, 1991.

Wasserman, Harvey and Norman Solomon. *Killing Our Own, The Disaster of America's Experience with Atomic Radiation.* New York: Dell Publishing Co. Inc., 1982.

Wintle, Bob. USS Wintle War Diary. [Online] www.wintle.com/de25/diary.htm.

10. The Wolfson Creek Breakwater

Bauer, Jim. Correspondence with John A. Campbell.

Bradley and Southern. Railway Era.

Clapp. Research.

The Dictionary of American Naval Fighting Ships, Volume V.

Hacking, Norman. "Old Ships Still Serve; As Breakwaters," *The Vancouver Province.*

Meunier, Roly. Interview with John A. Campbell.

Oyster Bay. [Online] www.northislandlinks.com/campbell_river/archives/oldsites/0999site/sites0999.html.

Phillips, Ed. Interview with John A. Campbell.

The Powell River Historical Museum.

Shields, Ed, Captain. *Salt of the Sea: The Pacific Coast Cod Fishery and the Last Days of Sail.* Surrey, BC, Heritage House Publishing Company Limited, 2001.

Twigg. *Union Steamships.*

Appendices

NorskeCanada.

The Powell River Historical Museum.

Haviland. "American Concrete Steamers."

Sawyer and Mitchell. *From America to United States.*

Grover. *U.S. Army Ships.*

Index

Index

About the type

The text in this book is set in ITC Cheltenham, designed by Tony Stan in 1975. It's heavier stroke weights, condensed proportions and a large x-height make it exceptionally legible.

Titles are set in Berthold's Akzidenz Grotesk, the precursor to today's oft-found Helvetica. It was designed by Günter Gerhard Lange. It provides a particularly clean, strong face. Incidentally, in German, *Akzidenz* means "trade type" and *Grotesk* means "sans serif."